The 52-Week Leadership Journey

A Collaborative Workbook for Purpose, Integrity, and Impact

By Andy Young

PLUCKY GROWTH

GROW YOUR DREAMS

For permission requests, write to the publisher at:

Plucky Growth LLC
Bay Village, OH
https://pluckygrowth.com

The 52-Week Leadership Journey: A Collaborative Workbook for Purpose, Integrity, and Impact

ISBN 979-8-9985856-0-9 (paperback)
ISBN 979-8-9985856-1-6 (e-book)

First edition

This is a work of non-fiction. The author has made every effort to ensure the accuracy of the information contained in this book; however, this book is not intended as legal, financial, or therapeutic advice. Readers should consult appropriate professionals for advice tailored to their situation.

Author's Note..5

Introduction:... 6

The Mindset and Qualities of Exceptional Leaders....................................6

    Week 1 - Developing a Growth Mindset (Carol Dweck)........................... 7

    Week 2 - The Power of Positive Thinking (Napoleon Hill)....................... 10

    Week 3 - Defining Your Purpose and Mission (Simon Sinek).................. 12

    Week 4 - Integrity and Leading by Example (Jocko Willink)................... 16

Part 1: Personal Excellence..19

    Week 5 - Self-Discipline and Overcoming Procrastination (Jocko Willink).....20

    Week 6 - Habits of Highly Effective People (Stephen Covey)................. 24

    Week 7 - Mastering Your Thoughts and Emotions (James Allen)............ 27

    Week 8 - Staying Motivated and Hungry (Les Brown)...........................31

    Week 9 - Continuous Learning and Skill Development......................... 34

    Week 10 - Health, Fitness and Energy Management.......................... 39

    Week 11 - Mental Toughness and Resilience (Navy SEALs)................. 43

    Week 12 - Time Management and Productivity (David Allen).................. 49

    Week 13 - Creativity and Idea Generation (James Webb Young)............ 53

Part 2:... 57

Leadership and Team Building... 57

    Week 14 - Traits of Exceptional Leaders (John Maxwell)......................58

    Week 15 - Servant Leadership (Robert Greenleaf)........................... 63

    Week 16 - Emotional Intelligence (Daniel Goleman)......................... 67

    Week 17 - Communication Skills (Dale Carnegie)............................ 72

    Week 18 - Building Trust and Psychological Safety (Patrick Lencioni)..... 77

    Week 19 - Giving Feedback and Performance Reviews...................... 82

    Week 20 - Conflict Resolution (Thomas-Kilmann)............................ 86

    Week 21 - Motivate and Inspire (Zig Ziglar)................................... 90

    Week 22 - Hiring A-Players (Geoff Smart)......................................93

    Week 23 - Team Dynamics and Collaboration................................. 97

    Week 24 - Celebrating Wins and Recognizing Excellence.................. 101

    Week 25 - After Action Reviews (Army Rangers)............................ 105

Part 3:... 109

Strategy and Execution..109

Week 26 - Crafting a Compelling Vision (John Kotter)..110

Week 27 - Goal Setting and Achieving BHAGs (Jim Collins)..114

Week 28 - Strategic Planning Best Practices..118

Week 29 - Agile Project Management (Jeff Sutherland)...124

Week 30 - Metrics, KPIs and Dashboards..127

Week 31 - Problem Solving Methodologies (McKinsey)...130

Week 32 - Decision Making Frameworks...134

Week 33 - Risk Management and Contingency Planning...138

Week 34 - Organizational Alignment (Patrick Lencioni)...142

Week 35 - Leading Change Initiatives (John Kotter)..146

Week 36 - Scaling Up Excellence (Robert Sutton)..150

Part 4:..**154**

Entrepreneurship and Innovation..**154**

Week 37 - Entrepreneurial Mindset (Seth Godin)...155

Week 38 - Lean Startup Principles (Eric Ries)...159

Week 39 - Business Model Generation (Alexander Osterwalder)..163

Week 40 - Blue Ocean Strategy (Renée Mauborgne)...167

Week 41 - Disruptive Innovation (Clayton Christensen)..171

Week 42 - Design Thinking (Tim Brown)...175

Week 43 - Jobs To Be Done Theory (Clayton Christensen)...180

Week 44 - Building Minimum Viable Products...185

Week 45 - Pitching and Storytelling (Nancy Duarte)...190

Week 46 - Negotiation Skills (Chris Voss)..196

Part 5:..**203**

Personal Development and Philosophy..**203**

Week 47 - Essentialism and Focusing on the Vital Few (Greg McKeown)..........................204

Week 48 - Principles and Mental Models (Ray Dalio)..209

Week 49 - Stoicism and the Art of Living (Ryan Holiday)...214

Week 50 - Logotherapy and Finding Meaning (Viktor Frankl)...221

Week 51 - The Slight Edge and Compound Effect (Jeff Olson)..226

Week 52 - Leaving a Legacy and Paying It Forward..232

Author's Note

Thanks for picking up this book. I have had the privilege of living through some unique challenges that ended up being huge opportunities, and along the way I've been able to meet numerous people and learn from them.

The result is a look at lessons I've learned along the way that have helped me lead a better life, and gain the freedom and resources to help others!

I've compiled these into this book.

The goal is for this book to be a workbook that you can use to grow yourself and people in your organizations. No one is an island when it comes to growth, so this is meant to be a journey you go on with others, but if you are someone who wants to go it alone, this book can help you grow too!

I'm sure there will be revisions and updates as I live through more experiences and learn more from others, but I do think that this is a wonderful first edition. I look forward to hearing the feedback and continue to improve it throughout the years to come.

Happy reading - and happy growing!

Introduction:

The Mindset and Qualities of Exceptional Leaders

Week 1 - Developing a Growth Mindset (Carol Dweck)

"Whether you think you can, or you think you can't—you're right." - Henry Ford

As a leader, your mindset is one of the most powerful tools you have. It shapes how you see yourself, your team, and the challenges you face. In this chapter, we'll explore the concept of growth mindset and how cultivating it can make you a more effective, resilient leader.

The term "growth mindset" was coined by psychologist Carol Dweck. In her groundbreaking book, *Mindset: The New Psychology of Success*, Dweck explains that individuals can be placed on a continuum according to their implicit views of where ability comes from. Those with a fixed mindset believe that abilities are mostly innate and unchangeable. Those with a growth mindset believe that abilities can be developed through dedication and hard work.

Video Break: The Power to Believe You Can Improve | Carol Dweck (10 min)

[https://www.youtube.com/watch?v=_X0mgOOSpLU]

Why does this matter for leaders? Leaders with a growth mindset see challenges as opportunities to learn and grow. They're not afraid to take risks or make mistakes, because they know that's how progress happens. They also foster a culture of development, encouraging their team members to keep learning and improving.

Let's look at an example. Imagine you're leading a project and you encounter a major setback. With a fixed mindset, you might think, "I'm not cut out for this," or "My team isn't capable of handling this." But with a growth mindset, you think, "This is an opportunity to learn and get better. We can figure this out."

Discussion (10-15 minutes)
- Ask participants to share their thoughts on the video/presentation
- Encourage them to reflect on their own mindset and how it has impacted their life and career
- Discuss how a growth mindset can be applied in their role as a leader
- Share examples of successful people or companies that embody a growth mindset

Developing a growth mindset isn't always easy, especially if you've had a fixed mindset for a long time. But the good news is that mindsets can be changed. It starts with awareness—paying attention to your self-talk and the way you respond to challenges.

One powerful tool is the "power of yet." When you find yourself thinking "I can't do this," add the word "yet" to the end of the sentence. "I can't do this yet, but I can learn." This small shift can make a big difference in how you approach difficulties.

Workshop: The "Power of Yet"

- Have participants identify an area where they feel stuck or have a fixed mindset (e.g. "I'm not good at public speaking")

- Ask them to reframe it using the power of yet (e.g. "I'm not good at public speaking yet, but I can improve with practice")

- Encourage them to set a small, achievable goal in that area for the coming week

As a leader, you can also model a growth mindset for your team. Share your own learning experiences and failures. Celebrate effort and progress, not just success. Create a safe environment for risk-taking and experimentation.

Remember, developing a growth mindset is an ongoing journey, not a destination. It requires consistent effort and practice. But the payoff—for you and your team—is immense. With a growth mindset, you can tackle bigger challenges, bounce back from setbacks, and ultimately achieve more than you ever thought possible.

Reflection Questions:

1. *Think about a recent challenge you faced as a leader. How might approaching it with a growth mindset have changed the outcome?*

2. *What's one area where you currently have a fixed mindset? How can you start to shift towards a growth mindset in that area?*

3. *How can you encourage a growth mindset in your team? What specific actions can you take this week to start building that culture?*

Week 2 - The Power of Positive Thinking (Napoleon Hill)

"Whatever the mind can conceive and believe, it can achieve." - Napoleon Hill

In the previous chapter, we explored the transformative power of a growth mindset. Building on that foundation, this chapter will dive into the power of positive thinking and how it can elevate your leadership and propel you towards your goals.

Napoleon Hill, the renowned author of *Think and Grow Rich*, dedicated his life to studying the habits of successful individuals. His work distills the common principles that these high achievers shared. At the heart of his philosophy is the idea that our thoughts have a direct and powerful impact on our reality.

Let's look at some of the key principles Hill identified:

1. **Definiteness of purpose:** Successful leaders have a clear, unwavering sense of their mission. They know exactly what they want to achieve and are laser-focused on that goal.

2. **Mastermind alliance:** No great leader operates in isolation. They surround themselves with a network of intelligent, capable individuals who support and challenge them.

3. **Going the extra mile:** Leaders who make a real impact are willing to put in more effort than what's expected. They consistently over-deliver and go above and beyond.

4. **Applied faith:** This isn't about religious faith, but rather a deep, unshakable belief in oneself and one's mission. Successful leaders maintain this faith even in the face of obstacles.

5. **Pleasing personality:** Leaders who attract followers and inspire loyalty tend to have engaging, likable personalities. They make others feel valued and appreciated.

As you reflect on these principles, consider how they show up (or could show up) in your own leadership. Perhaps you need to get clearer on your definiteness of purpose, or maybe you could benefit from building a stronger mastermind alliance.

One powerful way to embed these principles into your daily life is through the practice of affirmations. Affirmations are positive statements that you repeat to yourself, like "I am a confident and capable leader" or "I attract abundance and success." By consistently focusing your mind on these positive thoughts, you start to reshape your beliefs and behaviors.

Of course, positive thinking isn't about ignoring reality or denying challenges. It's about choosing to focus your energy on what you can control, and believing in your ability to overcome obstacles and achieve your goals.

As you go through your week, pay attention to your thought patterns. When you catch yourself slipping into negative self-talk, consciously shift your focus to something positive. Look for opportunities to apply Hill's principles in your leadership role.

Remember, developing a habit of positive thinking takes practice. Be patient with yourself and celebrate your progress along the way. As you continue to train your mind towards positivity, you'll be amazed at the impact it has on your leadership effectiveness and overall success.

Reflection Questions:

1. Which of Napoleon Hill's principles resonates most with you? Why?

2. Recall a time when positive thinking helped you overcome a leadership challenge. What did you learn from that experience?

3. What's one affirmation you can start using this week to boost your positive thinking?

Group Activity: (15 minutes)

- Divide participants into small groups
- Assign each group one of the principles to discuss
- Ask them to share examples of how they've seen this principle in action (or how they could apply it in their own leadership)
- Have each group share their key insights with the larger group

Individual Reflection: (5-10 minutes)

- Ask participants to identify one principle they want to focus on in the coming week
- Have them write down a specific action they will take to apply this principle
- Encourage them to share their commitment with a partner for accountability

Week 3 - Defining Your Purpose and Mission (Simon Sinek)

"People don't buy what you do; they buy why you do it." - Simon Sinek

In the last two chapters, we've explored the importance of mindset and positive thinking in leadership. Now, we'll dive into another crucial aspect: defining your purpose and mission.

Simon Sinek, author of *Start With Why* and a renowned expert on leadership, argues that the most inspiring leaders and organizations all think, act, and communicate in the same way – and it's the opposite of how most of us operate. They start with their "Why."

Video Break: _How Great Leaders Inspire Action_ | Simon Sinek (18 min)
[https://www.youtube.com/watch?v=qp0HIF3SfI4]

Your "Why" is your purpose, cause, or belief. It's the driving force behind everything you do. It's what inspires you and guides your decisions. When you clearly know your "Why," you have a foundation for leadership that is authentic, inspiring, and resilient.

Consider some of the world's most influential leaders – Martin Luther King Jr., Mahatma Gandhi, Nelson Mandela. They all had a clear sense of purpose that guided their actions and inspired others to follow them. Their "Why" was bigger than themselves.

So how do you find your "Why"?

It starts with deep self-reflection.

Ask yourself:

★ What are you passionate about?
★ What are your innate strengths?
★ Where do you add the greatest value?
★ How will you measure your life?

Your answers to these questions will start to reveal your "Why." It's not about what you do or how you do it, but the purpose behind it all.

Once you've defined your "Why," the next step is to align your actions and decisions with it. This is where the real power of "Start With Why" comes in. When you use your "Why" as a guidepost, it simplifies decision making and gives you a clear sense of direction.

It also makes you a more inspiring leader. When you communicate from your "Why," you tap into a deeper level of motivation and engagement. You inspire others to follow you not because they have to, but because they want to.

Of course, living and leading from your "Why" isn't always easy. It requires courage, conviction, and consistency. But the payoff – in terms of personal fulfillment, impact, and influence – is immense.

As you go through your week, take time to reflect on your "Why." Write it down and refine it. Start looking for ways to align your leadership with your purpose. Share your "Why" with your team and encourage them to find their own.

Remember, your "Why" is your most powerful leadership tool. When you lead from purpose, you not only inspire others – you inspire yourself. You tap into a wellspring of motivation and resilience that can carry you through even the toughest challenges.

Reflection Questions:

1. *What is your "Why"?*
    - *What gets you out of bed in the morning?*
    - *What are you passionate about?*
    - *How do you want to make a difference in the world?*

2. *Think about a leader you admire. Can you identify their "Why"? How does it inspire you?*

3. *How can you start aligning your daily leadership actions with your "Why"? What's one specific step you can take this week?*

Pair and Share: (10 minutes)

- Have participants pair up and share their reflections with each other
- Encourage them to ask questions and provide feedback to help each other refine their "Why" statements

Group Discussion: (10 minutes)

- Invite a few volunteers to share their "Why" with the larger group
- Discuss how a clear sense of purpose can guide decision making, inspire teams, and provide resilience in the face of challenges
- Brainstorm ways to communicate and embody one's "Why" in daily leadership

Week 4 - Integrity and Leading by Example (Jocko Willink)

"A leader must lead, but also be ready to follow. They must be aggressive, but not overbearing. A leader must be calm, but not robotic. They must be confident, but never cocky. A leader must be brave, but not foolhardy. They must have a competitive spirit, but be a gracious loser." - Jocko Willink

In the previous chapter, we explored the power of defining your purpose and mission. Now, we'll dive into another essential aspect of leadership: integrity and leading by example.

Jocko Willink, retired Navy SEAL commander and author of *Extreme Ownership*, emphasizes that leadership is about taking responsibility for everything in *your* world. This includes not just your actions, but also the actions of your team. It's about owning successes and failures alike.

At the heart of this ownership is integrity. Integrity means being honest, ethical, and consistent in your words and actions. It means doing the right thing, even when it's hard. As a leader, your integrity is the foundation of trust and respect with your team.

Consider some of the key principles of integrity in leadership:

1. **Taking ownership and responsibility:** Leaders with integrity don't make excuses or blame others. They take full responsibility for their decisions and actions.

2. **Being truthful and transparent:** Integrity means being honest, even when the truth is uncomfortable. It means being transparent about your intentions and expectations.

3. **Making ethical decisions:** Leaders with integrity make decisions based on their values and principles, not just on what's easy or expedient.

4. **Keeping promises and commitments:** Integrity means following through on what you say you'll do. It means being reliable and accountable.

But integrity isn't just about what you say – it's about what you do. This is where leading by example comes in. As a leader, your actions speak *louder* than your words. You set the tone and the standard for your team.

When you lead by example, you demonstrate your integrity in action. You show your team what it looks like to take ownership, to be honest, to make ethical decisions, and to keep commitments. You inspire them to do the same.

Case Study:

Sarah is the manager of a sales team at a large software company. Her team has been working hard to close a major deal with a new client, which would involve a significant customization of the company's software. The client has made it clear that they need the customization completed within a very tight timeframe.

As the project progresses, it becomes clear to Sarah that the timeframe is unrealistic. The customization is more complex than initially thought, and her team is already working overtime. She knows that rushing the project could lead to quality issues and ultimately damage the company's reputation.

However, Sarah's boss, the VP of Sales, is putting immense pressure on her to meet the deadline. He implies that if Sarah can't get it done, he'll find someone who can. He also suggests that Sarah should promise the client whatever they want to hear to close the deal, even if it's not entirely truthful.

Sarah is torn. She wants to please her boss and secure the deal for the company, but she also values her integrity and the trust of her team. She knows that making false promises to the client goes against her principles and could backfire in the long run.

As a leader, Sarah faces a tough decision.
- Should she prioritize the short-term gain of closing the deal, even if it means compromising her integrity?
- Or should she push back against her boss, risking his displeasure, in order to do what she believes is right for her team and the company in the long term?

Discussion Questions:

1. What are the key integrity issues in this scenario?

2. What would leading by example look like in this situation?

3. What actions should the leader take?

Of course, leading by example isn't always easy. It requires constant self-awareness and self-discipline. It means holding yourself to a higher standard. But the payoff – in terms of your team's trust, respect, and performance – is immense.

As you go through your week, consider your own leadership integrity. Are there areas where you could be more honest, more ethical, more accountable? Are you consistently leading by example?

Remember, your integrity is your most valuable leadership asset. Guard it fiercely. Demonstrate it daily. Use it to inspire and guide your team. When you lead with integrity, you create a culture of trust, respect, and high performance.

Reflection Questions:

1. *Think about a time when your integrity was tested as a leader. How did you respond? What did you learn?*

2. *Consider your current leadership role. Are there any areas where you could demonstrate more integrity? What specific actions could you take?*

3. *How can you encourage and support integrity in your team? What behaviors can you model and reinforce?*

Part 1: Personal Excellence

You can't lead others unless you can first lead yourself.

Week 5 - Self-Discipline and Overcoming Procrastination (Jocko Willink)

"Discipline equals freedom." - Jocko Willink

In the last chapter, we discussed the importance of integrity and leading by example. Now, we'll explore another critical aspect of effective leadership: self-discipline and overcoming procrastination.

Jocko Willink, retired Navy SEAL commander and author of *Discipline Equals Freedom: Field Manual,* argues that discipline is the path to true freedom. When you have the discipline to control your thoughts, emotions, and actions, you free yourself to achieve your full potential.

As a leader, self-discipline is particularly important. You set the standard for your team. If you lack discipline, it's hard to inspire it in others. Moreover, lack of discipline often manifests as procrastination – putting off important tasks, decisions, or conversations. Procrastination can quickly erode your effectiveness and credibility as a leader.

So how do you develop greater self-discipline and overcome procrastination? Here are some key principles and strategies:

1. **Take ownership of your time and actions.** Recognize that you are in control of how you spend your time and energy. Take responsibility for your choices and their consequences.

2. **Set and adhere to a routine.** Discipline is built through consistent, daily habits. Establish a routine that supports your goals and stick to it, even when you don't feel like it.

3. **Prioritize tasks and focus on execution.** Identify your most important tasks and tackle them first. Break large projects into smaller, manageable steps. Focus on executing consistently rather than waiting for perfect conditions.

4. **Develop mental toughness and resilience.** Discipline requires mental strength. Practice pushing through discomfort and doing what needs to be done, even when it's hard. Cultivate a mindset of resilience and determination.

Some Tools to add in your life:
- One practical technique for overcoming procrastination is the "time box" method. When you're procrastinating on a task, commit to working on it for a specific, short period of time (e.g., 25 minutes). Often, starting is the hardest part. Once you're in motion, momentum can carry you forward.

- Another strategy is the "2-minute rule." If a task will take less than two minutes, do it immediately. This helps prevent small tasks from piling up and overwhelming you.

- One other strategy to consider is the "eat the frog" strategy. When looking at a list of tasks, find the most difficult one and take care of it first.

As you go through your week, pay attention to your habits of discipline and procrastination.

- Where could you be more disciplined in your leadership?
- What tasks are you avoiding?

Practice applying the strategies above. Start small and build up your discipline muscle over time.

Remember, discipline is a practice, *not* a perfection. There will be days when you falter. The key is to get back on track and keep moving forward. As you develop greater self-discipline, you'll find that you're able to achieve more, lead more effectively, and experience greater freedom and fulfillment in your work and life.

Reflection Questions:

1. *What are your biggest procrastination triggers? How can you plan to deal with these triggers when they arise?*

2. *Think about a leader you admire. How do they demonstrate self-discipline? What can you learn from their example?*

3. *What's one area of your leadership where you could benefit from greater discipline? What specific steps will you take this week to strengthen your discipline in this area?*

Practical Activity:

Step 1: Take 30 minutes to set a specific, measurable goal related to improving your self-discipline or overcoming procrastination.

Step 2: Identify the key actions they will take to achieve this goal. When will you accomplish these actions?

Step 3: Write out a statement of you already having the goal in the present. (ie, By November 5, 2025, I, John Smith, am happy and grateful to own my home on the beach.)

Step 4: Post your timeline where you see it everyday and find someone to hold you accountable to your goal.

As we conclude this chapter, remember that self-discipline is like a muscle. The more you exercise it, the stronger it becomes. Every time you choose to do what needs to be done, even when you don't feel like it, you're strengthening your discipline muscle.

Developing self-discipline isn't always easy. It requires consistent effort and practice. There will be times when procrastination tempts you, when the easy path calls. These are the moments when your discipline is truly tested.

But here's the thing: every time you overcome procrastination, every time you choose discipline over comfort, you're not just getting the task done. You're training yourself to be a better leader. You're building the mental toughness and resilience that will serve you in countless situations. So here's my challenge to you: tackle your procrastination head-on. Don't wait for motivation to strike or conditions to be perfect. Choose discipline now. Start with one small task, one tiny habit. Build from there.

And remember, you're not in this alone. As a leader, one of your greatest resources is your team. Lean on each other for support and accountability. Share your goals and your struggles. Celebrate each other's victories. Together, you can create a culture of discipline that drives individual and collective success.

The path of discipline isn't always the easiest path, but it is the path to true freedom, effectiveness, and fulfillment. It's the path of great leaders. So keep strengthening that discipline muscle. Keep leading by example. Keep choosing the harder right over the easier wrong.

As Jocko Willink says, "Discipline equals freedom." Embrace the discipline, and unlock your full potential as a leader. The impact you'll make will be well worth the effort.

Week 6 - Habits of Highly Effective People (Stephen Covey)

"We are what we repeatedly do. Excellence, then, is not an act, but a habit." - Aristotle

In the early 1900s, a young journalist named Napoleon Hill was given an assignment by the wealthy businessman Andrew Carnegie. Carnegie challenged Hill to interview the most successful people of the time and distill their secrets into a formula for success. Hill accepted the challenge, and over the next two decades, he studied and interviewed hundreds of the world's most effective individuals.

One of the key insights Hill gleaned from his research was the power of habits. The highly effective people he studied weren't just lucky or naturally gifted. They had developed specific habits that allowed them to consistently perform at a high level.

This insight was later echoed and expanded upon by Stephen Covey in his seminal book, *The 7 Habits of Highly Effective People*. Covey argued that true effectiveness comes from aligning our habits with universal principles. He identified seven such habits:

1. Be Proactive
Being proactive means taking responsibility for your life and your choices. Rather than reacting to external circumstances, proactive people focus on what they can control. They take initiative, anticipate problems, and seek solutions. As a leader, being proactive means setting the agenda, making things happen, and inspiring others to do the same.

2. Begin with the End in Mind
Beginning with the end in mind means having a clear vision of your desired direction and destination. It's about defining your mission and values, and then aligning your actions accordingly. Effective leaders have a strong sense of purpose. They communicate a compelling vision and help their teams see how their work fits into the larger picture.

3. Put First Things First
Putting first things first is about prioritization and time management. It means focusing on important, non-urgent activities that align with your mission and values. Effective leaders don't get caught up in the tyranny of the urgent. They plan their time around their priorities, delegate effectively, and ensure that their team is focused on the most important goals.

4. Think Win-Win

Thinking win-win is about seeking mutual benefit in all interactions. It's a mindset of abundance and cooperation, rather than scarcity and competition. Effective leaders build strong, trusting relationships. They look for ways to create value for all stakeholders. They negotiate fairly and seek outcomes that benefit the whole team or organization.

5. Seek First to Understand, Then to Be Understood

This habit is about empathetic communication. It means listening with the intent to truly understand the other person's perspective, feelings, and needs, before seeking to be understood yourself. Effective leaders are excellent listeners. They ask questions, seek to understand different viewpoints, and communicate with clarity and respect.

6. Synergize

Synergizing is about creative cooperation. It means valuing differences and finding innovative solutions that are better than any individual could have come up with alone. Effective leaders cultivate a culture of teamwork and continuous improvement. They bring out the best in others and create teams that are more than the sum of their parts.

7. Sharpen the Saw

Sharpening the saw is about continuous self-renewal in all four dimensions of life: physical, social/emotional, mental, and spiritual. It means taking care of yourself so that you can perform at your best. Effective leaders lead by example in terms of self-care. They invest in their own learning and growth, and they encourage their teams to do the same.

Developing these habits is a lifelong journey. It requires self-awareness, discipline, and consistent practice. But the payoff, in terms of personal and professional effectiveness, is immense.

Activity:

Grab a sheet of paper and write down each of the 7 habits above. Next to each habit write down:
- What does this habit mean in practice (how would it look, or manifest, in my life)?
- How can this habit make someone a better leader?
- What are some challenges that you would face implementing this habit in your life, and how could you overcome them?

As you go through your week, reflect on each of these habits. Which ones are already strengths for you? Which ones could use more attention and development? Choose one habit to focus on each week. Look for opportunities to practice it in your leadership role.

Remember, as Aristotle said, *excellence is a habit.*

By consistently practicing these seven habits, you can develop the skills and character of a truly effective leader. You can make a positive impact not just on your own life, but on the lives of those you lead and serve.

Reflection Questions:

1. *Think about a highly effective leader you know or admire. Which of the seven habits do they embody? How does this contribute to their effectiveness?*

2. *Consider a recent leadership challenge you faced. How might applying one or more of the seven habits have changed your approach or the outcome?*

3. *Which of the seven habits do you feel is your strongest? Which one do you most need to work on? What specific steps can you take this week to strengthen this habit?*

Week 7 - Mastering Your Thoughts and Emotions (James Allen)

"The outer conditions of a person's life will always be found to be harmoniously related to his inner state...Men do not attract that which they want, but that which they are."
- James Allen

Last week, we explored the seven habits of highly effective people, learning how aligning our habits with universal principles can transform our leadership and lives. Building on this foundation, this week we're diving into another crucial aspect of personal and leadership development: mastering our thoughts and emotions. Our inner world has a profound impact on our outer reality, influencing not just our own well-being and performance, but also the morale and productivity of our teams. In this chapter, we'll explore the wisdom of James Allen's classic book, *As a Man Thinketh*, which introduces the powerful idea that our thoughts shape our character, circumstances, and destinies. We'll learn strategies for becoming more aware of our mental and emotional patterns, reframing negative thoughts into positive ones, and cultivating a leadership mindset of resilience, optimism, and growth. By taking responsibility for our thoughts and emotions, we tap into a wellspring of inner peace, clarity, and strength that can transform our leadership impact and our lives.

In 1903, a little-known English writer named James Allen published a small book that would go on to become a classic in the field of personal development. The book, titled *As a Man Thinketh*, introduced a simple but profound idea: our thoughts shape our reality.

Allen argued that our minds are like gardens, and our thoughts are the seeds. We can choose to plant seeds of positivity, wisdom, and growth, or we can allow our gardens to be overrun with the weeds of negativity, fear, and limitation. The choice is ours, and the consequences are far-reaching.

As leaders, the state of our inner world is particularly important. Our thoughts and emotions not only influence our own well-being and effectiveness, but they also have a ripple effect on our teams and organizations. If we're constantly stressed, anxious, or reactive, that energy will permeate our leadership style and our team's culture.

On the other hand, if we cultivate a mindset of calmness, resilience, and optimism, we'll be better equipped to navigate challenges, inspire others, and create a positive work environment. This is why mastering our thoughts and emotions is a critical skill for any leader.

So how do we do this? It starts with self-awareness. We need to become conscious of our mental and emotional patterns. What thoughts do we tend to dwell on? How do we typically react to stress or adversity? What triggers our negative emotions?

One powerful tool for developing self-awareness is mindfulness meditation. By taking time each day to sit quietly and observe our thoughts and emotions without judgment, we can start to gain more insight and control over our inner world.

Another key strategy is reframing. Often, our thoughts and emotions are based on our interpretations of events, rather than the events themselves. By learning to reframe challenges as opportunities, failures as lessons, and obstacles as chances to grow, we can shift our emotional state and our leadership impact.

It's also important to cultivate practices that promote positive thoughts and emotions. This can include things like gratitude journaling, positive self-talk, and surrounding ourselves with uplifting influences.

Application Activity:

1. **Read through this quote:**

   "Mind is the Master power that moulds and makes, And Man is Mind, and evermore he takes The tool of Thought, and, shaping what he wills, Brings forth a thousand joys, a thousand ills: —He thinks in secret, and it comes to pass: Environment is but his looking-glass." - James Allen, As a Man Thinketh

2. **Consider these concepts from James Allen:**

   a. Our thoughts shape our reality.

   b. We have the power to control our thoughts and thus, our lives.

   c. Our character is the complete sum of all our thoughts.

(Continued on next page)

3. **Grab a sheet of paper to jot down your thoughts and notes on while you answer these questions:**

   a. Explain the connection between thoughts, emotions, and leadership effectiveness.

   b. Think of a few strategies for managing thoughts and emotions, such as mindfulness, reframing, and self-reflection.

Of course, mastering our thoughts and emotions is a lifelong journey. There will always be new challenges, new triggers, and new opportunities for growth. The key is to approach this journey with patience, self-compassion, and a commitment to continuous learning.

As you go through your week, pay attention to your inner world. Notice your thoughts and emotions, and observe how they impact your leadership presence and decisions. When you find yourself in a negative or reactive state, take a step back. Breathe. Reframe. Choose a more positive and productive path forward.

Remember, as James Allen said, "You are today where your thoughts have brought you; you will be tomorrow where your thoughts take you." By mastering your thoughts and emotions, you master your leadership potential. You become the kind of leader who not only weathers storms, but who also guides others to calmer, clearer waters.

Reflection Questions:

1. *Think about a recent situation where your emotions got the best of you. How did it impact your leadership effectiveness? What could you have done differently?*

2. *What are some of your most common negative thought patterns? How can you start to reframe these thoughts in a more positive and productive way?*

3. *What practices can you incorporate into your daily routine to cultivate more positive thoughts and emotions? How can you make these practices a consistent part of your leadership lifestyle?*

Meditation & Journaling Activity

Meditation Practice and Guidance

- Find a comfortable seated position, close your eyes, and focus on your breath.
- Observe your thoughts and emotions without judgment, and practice letting your thoughts pass without attachment.
- End the meditation, after 5 or so minutes to start, by setting an intention for how you want to manage your thoughts and emotions in your leadership role

Journaling Exercise

- Write down your reflections on the meditation experience.
- Prompts to consider:
    - What thoughts and emotions did you observe?
    - How do these thoughts and emotions typically impact your leadership?
    - What strategies can you use to better manage your thoughts and emotions?

Taking time to think and "garden" your thoughts is time very well spent. Be sure to make time in your schedule to form this habit - and make it a high priority!

Week 8 - Staying Motivated and Hungry (Les Brown)

"You must take action now that will move you towards your goals. Develop a sense of urgency in your life." - Les Brown

Last week, we explored the profound impact of our thoughts and emotions on our leadership and lives. We learned that by mastering our inner world, we can tap into a powerful source of clarity, resilience, and strength. This week, we're building on that foundation by diving into another crucial aspect of personal and leadership development: staying motivated and hungry.

In the world of personal development, few voices ring out with as much passion and power as that of Les Brown. Born in an abandoned building and labeled "educable mentally retarded" as a child, Brown went on to become one of the most influential motivational speakers of our time. His message is simple but profound: to achieve great things, you must be hungry.

Video Break: You Gotta Be Hungry | Les Brown (7 min)
[https://www.youtube.com/watch?v=1dWfwh-Rgzo]

Optional/Extra Credit: It's Not Over Until You Win | Les Brown (30 min)
[https://www.youtube.com/watch?v=8Fd06U-3TAY]

But what does it mean to be hungry? It's not about physical hunger, but about an insatiable drive to learn, grow, and achieve. It's about having a clear vision of what you want and being willing to do whatever it takes to get there. It's about pushing yourself beyond your comfort zone, embracing challenges as opportunities, and never settling for mediocrity.

As leaders, this kind of hunger is essential. It's what allows us to set bold goals, to inspire others to follow us, and to persevere through setbacks and obstacles. But staying hungry isn't always easy. In the face of daily pressures and routines, it's all too common for our motivation to wane and our passion to fade.

That's why it's crucial to have strategies for reigniting and sustaining our motivation. One key is to keep our goals front and center. Write them down, visualize them, and break them down into actionable steps. Celebrate your progress along the way, and use each milestone as a springboard to the next.

Another strategy is to surround yourself with positive influences. Seek out mentors, role models, and accountability partners who will inspire you, challenge you, and keep you on track. Immerse yourself in motivational books, podcasts, and videos. Attend workshops and conferences that energize you and expand your thinking.

It's also important to embrace failure as a necessary part of growth. As Les Brown often says, "Fail your way to success." Don't let setbacks discourage you - instead, use them as lessons and stepping stones. Cultivate a mindset of resilience and determination, and keep pushing forward no matter what.

Question Break:

- What resonated with you most from Les Brown's message?
- What are some common obstacles to staying motivated, and how can they be overcome?

Of course, staying motivated isn't just about individual success - it's also about inspiring and uplifting others. As a leader, one of your most important roles is to be a source of motivation for your team. This means communicating a clear and compelling vision, recognizing and celebrating achievements, and creating an environment where everyone feels challenged and supported to give their best.

- *How can you, as a leader, inspire and sustain motivation in your team?*

As you go through your week, take time to reflect on your own level of motivation and hunger. Are you setting goals that truly excite and stretch you? Are you surrounding yourself with influences that lift you up? Are you using setbacks as fuel for growth? And are you passing that spark of motivation on to others?

Remember, as Les Brown says, "You have greatness within you." By staying motivated and hungry, you tap into that greatness and become the kind of leader who not only achieves extraordinary things, but who also inspires others to do the same. So keep feeding your hunger, keep stoking your fire, and keep reaching for your highest potential. Your leadership journey is just beginning.

Reflection Questions:

1. *Think about a time when you were at your most motivated and driven. What fueled that hunger? How can you recreate those conditions in your current role?*

2. *Who are the people in your life who inspire and motivate you? How can you surround yourself with more positive influences and support systems?*

Re-envision your Goals:

Grab the goal sheet you made in Week 5

Look over your goals and see if you want to change/alter/add to any of your goals.

Re-examine how you will reach those goals, are you making progress on the steps you set out to achieve? If not, what steps can be altered based on your hunger?

For each step, you will want to identify:
- Potential obstacles and how you will overcome them
- How you will celebrate progress and maintain momentum
- How you will hold yourself accountable

Take any updates and share them with your accountability person and explain the reason for the changes.

Week 9 - Continuous Learning and Skill Development

"Live as if you were to die tomorrow. Learn as if you were to live forever." - Mahatma Gandhi

Last week, we explored the importance of staying motivated and hungry in our leadership journey. We learned that maintaining a strong drive is essential for achieving our goals and inspiring others. This week, we're building on that foundation by diving into another crucial aspect of leadership excellence: continuous learning and skill development.

In today's rapidly changing world, the ability to learn and adapt is more important than ever. As leaders, we must not only keep pace with evolving technologies, strategies, and best practices, but also stay ahead of the curve. The most effective leaders are those who embrace a mindset of lifelong learning, constantly seeking new knowledge and skills to enhance their leadership capabilities.

But what does it mean to be a lifelong learner? It's not just about accumulating degrees or certifications. It's about cultivating a genuine curiosity about the world around us. It's about being open to new ideas and perspectives, even when they challenge our existing beliefs. It's about seeing every experience - whether success or failure - as an opportunity to learn and grow.

One key to effective learning is self-awareness. We must be honest with ourselves about our strengths and weaknesses, and identify the skills we need to develop to achieve our goals. This might involve technical skills specific to our industry, or it might be softer skills like emotional intelligence, communication, or strategic thinking. Take a moment to fill in the chart below.

Application Activity:

Current Strengths	Current Areas for Improvement

Pick 2-3 skills you would like to develop over the next 6-12 months.
Think about skills that would enhance your leadership effectiveness and align with your career goals.

1. _____

2. _____

3. _____

Once we've identified our learning needs, the next step is to create a personal development plan. This plan should outline specific skills we want to develop, why they're important, and how we intend to acquire them. It might involve formal education, online courses, reading books, attending workshops, seeking mentorship, or simply practicing new skills in our daily work.

It's also important to understand our own learning style. Some of us are visual learners, others are auditory or kinesthetic. By understanding how we learn best, we can choose learning strategies that are most effective for us. For example, a visual learner might benefit more from diagrams and charts, while an auditory learner might prefer podcasts or lectures.

Another powerful learning strategy is peer learning. By connecting with others who are on a similar learning journey, we can share insights, challenge each other's thinking, and hold each other accountable. This might involve joining a professional learning community, finding a learning partner, or participating in group discussions and workshops.

As leaders, our commitment to learning sets the tone for our entire organization. When we model curiosity and a growth mindset, we create a culture where learning is valued and encouraged. This not only enhances our own effectiveness but also helps to develop the next generation of leaders within our organization.

Remember, learning is not a destination, but a journey. There will always be new skills to acquire, new challenges to overcome, and new horizons to explore. By embracing continuous learning, we ensure that we're always growing, always improving, and always ready to lead in an ever-changing world.

As you go through your week, take time to reflect on your own learning journey. What new skills or knowledge would enhance your leadership effectiveness? How can you create more opportunities for learning in your daily work? And how can you inspire a love of learning in those you lead?

Reflection Questions:

1. *What are the top three skills you'd like to develop in the next year? How would these skills enhance your leadership effectiveness?*

2. *Think about a recent learning experience that was particularly impactful. What made it so effective? How can you apply those lessons to future learning opportunities?*

3. *How can you create a culture of continuous learning within your team or organization? What specific actions can you take to model and encourage lifelong learning?*

Creating your Personal Development Plan

Review each of the skills you listed earlier as areas you would want to improve. Then answer these questions:

- Why is this skill important to my leadership and career development?
- What specific learning activities will I undertake (courses, workshops, books, mentoring, etc.)
- When will I have this skill acquired by, or finish this plan by?
- How will I apply and practice the skill in my current role?

Your plan should be realistic and ACTIONABLE. To make an amazing plan and never act on it, would be way worse than to make a small plan and accomplish it.

What is your Learning Style?

Earlier in the chapter we discussed learning styles briefly. Knowing your learning style is not only necessary, but a very easy advantage to gain in the path of improvement. While everyone can learn through various methods, most people have a preferred style that allows them to absorb and retain information more easily. The three primary learning styles are:

1. **Visual Learners:** These individuals learn best through seeing. They prefer visual aids like charts, graphs, diagrams, and written instructions.

2. **Auditory Learners:** These learners absorb information best through hearing. They benefit from lectures, discussions, and verbal explanations.

3. **Kinesthetic Learners:** Also known as tactile learners, these individuals learn best through doing. They prefer hands-on experiences, physical activities, and practical applications.

Understanding your dominant learning style can help you optimize your learning experiences.

For example:

➤ If you're a **visual learner**, you might benefit from creating mind maps, using color-coded notes, or watching educational videos.

➤ If you're an **auditory learner**, you might find podcasts, group discussions, or recording and listening to your own notes particularly helpful.

➤ If you're a **kinesthetic learner,** you might learn best through role-playing, hands-on experiments, or applying concepts in real-world scenarios.

It's important to note that most people use a combination of these styles, and can develop skills in their non-dominant styles. By understanding your preferences, you can choose learning strategies that play to your strengths while also working to improve in other areas.

★ **What learning style do you think is your preferred method?**

★ **What learning style do you think is your second preference?**

By identifying your preferred style, you can tailor your learning approach and maximize your growth potential.

Remember, the goal is not to limit yourself to one style, but to leverage your strengths while developing a well-rounded approach to learning. This self-awareness will not only enhance your personal development but also make you a more effective leader as you help others identify and leverage their own learning styles.

Week 10 - Health, Fitness and Energy Management

"To keep the body in good health is a duty... otherwise we shall not be able to keep our mind strong and clear." - Buddha

Last week, we explored the importance of continuous learning and skill development in our leadership journey. This week, we turn our attention to an often overlooked but crucial aspect of leadership effectiveness: our physical health and energy management.

As leaders, we often focus on developing our mental and emotional capabilities, but we sometimes neglect the very foundation upon which these capacities rest - our physical well-being. The truth is, our health and fitness levels have a profound impact on our ability to lead effectively. They influence our energy levels, our mental clarity, our emotional resilience, and even our decision-making abilities.

Consider this:

- How effective can you be as a leader if you're constantly tired, stressed, or battling health issues?

- How can you inspire and motivate others if you lack the energy to fully engage with your team?

The answer is clear - to be at our best as leaders, we must prioritize our health and fitness.

Let's break this down into four key areas:

1. **Nutrition:** The food we eat directly affects our energy levels and cognitive function. A balanced diet rich in whole foods, lean proteins, and healthy fats can improve focus, mood, and overall well-being. As leaders, we need to fuel our bodies properly to perform at our best.

2. **Exercise:** Regular physical activity not only improves our physical health but also boosts our mental acuity and emotional resilience. Exercise releases endorphins, reduces stress, and improves sleep quality - all of which contribute to better leadership performance.

3. **Sleep:** Quality sleep is essential for cognitive function, emotional regulation, and physical recovery. Chronic sleep deprivation can impair judgment, decrease productivity,

and increase stress levels. As leaders, we need to prioritize getting enough quality sleep to maintain our effectiveness.

4. **Stress Management:** While some stress can be motivating, chronic stress can be detrimental to our health and leadership abilities. Effective stress management techniques, such as meditation, deep breathing, or regular breaks, can help us maintain our composure and make better decisions under pressure.

To improve in these areas, start by conducting a personal energy audit.

Assess your current habits in each of these four areas. Where are you doing well? Where could you improve? Be honest with yourself - this is the first step towards positive change. You can use the chart below to help:

Current Habits	Rating (1-10, 10 as best)	Areas of Improvement
Sleep		
Nutrition		
Exercise		
Stress Management		
Personal Development/Study		
Other		
Other		

Next, set specific, achievable goals for improvement. Perhaps you want to incorporate more vegetables into your diet, start a regular exercise routine, establish a consistent sleep schedule, or practice daily meditation. Remember, small, consistent changes often lead to the most sustainable results.

Application Activity:

★ What is one health or fitness goal you would like to achieve?

★ What is an obstacle you will face?

★ Develop a strategy on overcoming those obstacles.

As you work towards these goals, be prepared for obstacles. Time constraints, work pressures, and old habits can all challenge your new health-focused lifestyle. The key is to anticipate these challenges and develop strategies to overcome them. This might involve meal prepping for busy weeks, scheduling workouts like important meetings, or enlisting an accountability partner to keep you on track.

Remember, as a leader, your commitment to health and fitness sets an example for your entire team. When you prioritize your well-being, you give others permission to do the same. This can lead to a healthier, more energized, and more productive work environment overall.

As you go through your week, pay attention to how your physical state affects your leadership. Notice how your energy levels, mood, and decision-making abilities fluctuate based on your health habits. Use these observations as motivation to continue investing in your well-being.

Reflection Questions:

1. *Pick one specific habit you would like to improve. What are three concrete steps you WILL take in the next week to work on improving that habit?*

2. *Think about a time when you were at your physical best. How did this impact your leadership effectiveness?*

3. *How can changes you make today help improve your 5, 10, 20, and 50 years-in-the-future self?*

Remember, your health is your most valuable asset as a leader. By prioritizing your physical well-being, you're not just investing in yourself - you're investing in your ability to lead, inspire, and make a positive impact in the world.

Week 11 - Mental Toughness and Resilience (Navy SEALs)

"The only easy day was yesterday." - Navy SEAL motto

Last week, we explored the critical importance of physical health and energy management in leadership. This week, we turn our attention to an equally vital aspect of leadership effectiveness: mental toughness and resilience. To guide us in this exploration, we'll draw inspiration from one of the most mentally and physically demanding training programs in the world - that of the Navy SEALs.

Breathe like a SEAL

SEALs use a special breathing method to help them cope with high stress environments - it is called box breathing. Here is how it is done:

- Breathe in through your nose for the count of four
- Hold your breath for a count of four
- Breathe out through your mouth forcefully for a count of four
- Leave your lungs empty for a count of four
- Repeat for a few rounds, or until you feel yourself more relaxed and calm.

Box breathing can help manage stress and improve focus, it is an invaluable tool to have in your kit, and can - and should - be used frequently throughout the day.

The Navy SEALs are renowned for their ability to perform under extreme pressure, to push past perceived limits, and to maintain composure in chaotic situations. While most of us will never face the life-or-death scenarios that SEALs routinely encounter, the principles they use to build mental toughness can be powerfully applied in our leadership roles.

Let's start by considering the Navy SEAL Creed:

> In times of war or uncertainty there is a special breed of warrior ready to answer our Nation's call. A common man with an uncommon desire to succeed. Forged by adversity, he stands alongside America's finest special operations forces to serve his country, the American people, and protect their way of life. I am that man.
>
> **My Trident is a symbol of honor and heritage.** Bestowed upon me by the heroes that have gone before, it embodies the trust of those I have sworn to protect. By wearing the

Trident I accept the responsibility of my chosen profession and way of life. It is a privilege that I must earn every day.

My loyalty to Country and Team is beyond reproach. I humbly serve as a guardian to my fellow Americans, always ready to defend those who are unable to defend themselves. I do not advertise the nature of my work, nor seek recognition for my actions. I voluntarily accept the inherent hazards of my profession, placing the welfare and security of others before my own.

I serve with honor on and off the battlefield. The ability to control my emotions and my actions, regardless of circumstance, sets me apart from other men. Uncompromising integrity is my standard. My character and honor are steadfast. My word is my bond.

We expect to lead and be led. In the absence of orders I will take charge, lead my teammates and accomplish the mission. I lead by example in all situations.

I will never quit. I persevere and thrive on adversity. My Nation expects me to be physically harder and mentally stronger than my enemies. If knocked down, I will get back up, every time. I will draw on every remaining ounce of strength to protect my teammates and to accomplish our mission. I am never out of the fight.

We demand discipline. We expect innovation. The lives of my teammates and the success of our mission depend on me – my technical skill, tactical proficiency, and attention to detail. My training is never complete.

We train for war and fight to win. I stand ready to bring the full spectrum of combat power to bear in order to achieve my mission and the goals established by my country. The execution of my duties will be swift and violent when required yet guided by the very principles that I serve to defend.

Brave men have fought and died building the proud tradition and feared reputation that I am bound to uphold. In the worst of conditions, the legacy of my teammates steadies my resolve and silently guides my every deed. I will not fail.

Exercise: The 40% Rule in Leadership

Introduction:
The 40% Rule, popularized by Navy SEAL David Goggins, states that when you think you're done and have reached your limit, you're actually only about 40% of what you're truly capable of. This principle encourages pushing beyond perceived limits and tapping into hidden reserves of strength and endurance.

Part 1: Understanding the 40% Rule
Reflect on a time when you pushed past what you thought was your limit.

1. What made you think you had reached your limit?
2. What motivated you to keep going?
3. How did you feel after pushing past your perceived limit?

Part 2: Case Study

Lily, a project manager at a tech startup, is leading a critical product launch. Her team has been working long hours for weeks, and morale is low. With just two days left before the launch, a major bug is discovered that threatens to derail the entire project. Lily's team is exhausted and feels they've reached their limit. Many are suggesting they should delay the launch.

Lily remembers the 40% Rule. She realizes that while her team feels they've hit their limit, they likely have more to give. She decides to rally her team for one final push.

Lily breaks down the remaining work into smaller, manageable tasks. She acknowledges the team's hard work and reminds them of the project's importance. She also implements short, frequent breaks to help maintain focus and energy.

To everyone's surprise, the team not only fixes the bug but also implements additional improvements they hadn't thought possible. They launch on time, and the product is a huge success.

Application Questions:

1. How did Lily apply the 40% Rule in this situation?

2. What specific strategies did Lily use to help her team push past their perceived limits?

3. Think about a challenging situation in your own leadership experience. How could applying the 40% Rule have changed your approach or the outcome?

4. What are some potential risks or downsides of applying the 40% Rule? How can leaders balance pushing limits with avoiding burnout?

5. How can you incorporate the 40% Rule into your daily leadership practice? Give specific examples.

Conclusion:

The 40% Rule is not about pushing people to exhaustion, but about helping them realize their untapped potential. Effective use of this principle involves balancing challenge with support, and always prioritizing the well-being of your team.

The Navy SEAL creed embodies the mental toughness, resilience, and unwavering commitment that define Navy SEALs. While our leadership challenges may be different, we can draw valuable lessons from their approach:

1. **Embrace adversity:** SEALs view challenges as opportunities for growth. As leaders, we can reframe obstacles as chances to learn and improve.

2. **Control emotions and actions:** The ability to remain calm under pressure is crucial for effective leadership.

3. **Lead by example:** SEALs expect to both lead and be led. Great leaders inspire through their actions.

4. **Never quit:** Persistence in the face of difficulty is a hallmark of mental toughness.

5. **Continuous improvement:** SEALs believe their training is never complete. As leaders, we should always strive to learn and grow.

6. **Discipline and innovation:** Balancing structure with creativity is key to adaptable leadership.

7. **Uphold a legacy:** SEALs are driven by the reputation they must uphold. As leaders, we should consider the legacy we're creating.

By incorporating these principles into our leadership approach, we can develop the mental toughness and resilience needed to navigate challenges and inspire our teams to greatness.

Reflection Questions:

1. *Which aspect of the SEAL Creed resonates most with you as a leader? Why?*

2. *Think of a recent leadership challenge. How could applying SEAL principles have improved your response?*

3. *What's one specific way you can build mental toughness in your daily leadership practice?*

Remember, mental toughness isn't about being tough in the traditional sense. It's about developing the resilience, focus, and determination to lead effectively, no matter the circumstances. By cultivating these qualities, we become leaders who can guide our teams through any challenge.

Personal Resilience Plan

A personal resilience plan offers several key benefits for leaders:

1. Increased self-awareness: Creating a resilience plan requires you to reflect on your strengths, weaknesses, and typical responses to stress. This self-awareness is crucial for effective leadership.
2. Proactive stress management: By identifying potential challenges and planning coping strategies in advance, you're better equipped to handle stress when it arises.
3. Improved decision-making: A resilience plan helps you maintain clarity and focus during difficult times, leading to better decision-making under pressure.

4. <u>Enhanced performance:</u> By building your resilience, you're able to maintain high performance even in challenging situations.
5. <u>Faster recovery:</u> With a plan in place, you can bounce back more quickly from setbacks and failures.

A personal resilience plan is a powerful tool for developing the mental toughness needed to thrive as a leader in challenging environments.**Here are some questions to help you get started on yours:**

- What are the 2-3 biggest leadership challenges for you that require mental toughness?

- What specific mental toughness techniques will you apply?

- How will you ensure that you practice these techniques regularly?

At this point you are starting to develop a number of goals, plans, and procedures. Take a trip to an office supply store and get a 3-ring binder. Print off your plans and start to place and organize them into the binder. **You are creating your Personal Leadership Field Manual (PLFM)!**

Week 12 - Time Management and Productivity (David Allen)

"Your mind is for having ideas, not holding them." - David Allen

In our previous chapter, we explored the importance of mental toughness and resilience in leadership. This week, we turn our attention to another critical skill for effective leaders: time management and productivity. To guide us in this exploration, we'll draw on the wisdom of David Allen, creator of the Getting Things Done (GTD) methodology.

In today's fast-paced, information-rich world, leaders are constantly bombarded with tasks, ideas, and responsibilities. Without an effective system for managing this influx, it's easy to become overwhelmed, stressed, and ultimately less productive. This is where Allen's GTD system comes in.

At its core, GTD is about creating mental space. Allen argues that our minds are for generating ideas, not storing them. By creating a trusted system outside of our minds to capture and organize our tasks and commitments, we free up mental energy for creative thinking, problem-solving, and strategic planning - the high-value activities that truly drive leadership effectiveness.

Let's break down the key principles of GTD:

1. **Capture:** Collect everything that has your attention - tasks, ideas, commitments - into a trusted system outside your mind. This could be a notebook, a digital app, or any tool you trust and will use consistently.

2. **Clarify:** Process what you've captured. Decide what each item means and what action, if any, it requires. Is it actionable? If so, what's the next step? If not, is it reference material to be filed, or can it be discarded?

3. **Organize:** Put everything in its right place. Create a system of lists and categories that make sense for you. This might include project lists, a calendar for time-specific commitments, and a "someday/maybe" list for ideas you're not ready to act on yet.

4. **Reflect:** Regularly review your system. A weekly review is a cornerstone of GTD. Use this time to update your lists, review your calendar, and ensure your system is current and complete.

5. **Engage:** Use your system to guide your actions. Trust in your organization and prioritization to focus on the right tasks at the right time.

Extra Resources for GTD

Video Break: The Secret Weapon, Using Evernote as a Powerhouse Second Brain (7 min)
[https://www.youtube.com/watch?v=_sTMZwlsCJk]

You can read more about **The Secret Weapon** here: https://thesecretweapon.org

Getting in Control and Creating Space | David Allen (17 min)
[https://www.youtube.com/watch?v=kOSFxKaqOm4]

One powerful practice within GTD is the concept of "Inbox Zero." This doesn't necessarily mean having an empty email inbox at all times, but rather processing your inputs regularly and completely. When you see an email or receive a piece of information, decide immediately what to do with it. Act on it, delegate it, file it for reference, or delete it. This practice alone can significantly reduce stress and increase productivity.

Another key element is the *Weekly Review*. This is a dedicated time to step back, review your commitments and projects, and ensure you're on track. It's a chance to celebrate progress, adjust priorities, and prepare for the week ahead. Many leaders find this practice transformative, as it provides a sense of control and clarity that carries through to all aspects of their work.

Build your Weekly Review

I often find myself starting to think about tasks or pending items on Saturdays. This could have the potential to derail my whole weekend and rob me of the opportunity to enjoy my time fully. When those robbing thoughts start to creep in, I remember that I should lean into the process of my Weekly Review - and then they are quickly quieted.

Here are the key points I use in my weekly review:

Get Clear
- → Collect loose papers and materials
- → Get Inbox to zero
- → Empty your head

Get Current
- → Review Action Lists
- → Review past calendar data
- → Review upcoming calendar
- → Review Waiting For list
- → Review Project (and larger outcome) lists
- → Review any relevant checklists

Get Creative
- → Review Someday/Maybe items or lists
- → Be creative and courageous
- → Read over Journal from same week last year, this week or random entries for inspiration and motivation

0-15 minutes: Clean up email/paper notes. Interview notes, new contacts, and emails I want to follow up on all get filed. If there's a message I can fire a response to in a minute or two, I'll respond, but nothing that requires research.

15-45 minutes: Review ideas, projects, calendar appointments. This is where I spend the bulk of my time. I look through my idea bank, trash anything stale, add new ideas, and assign dates where I can. I head over to my to-do app, clear out old and completed tasks, and add new or follow-up items based on my calendar, assignments, and trigger list.

45-60 minutes: Brainstorming. This is where I head back to my idea bank and start brainstorming topics I want to write or learn more about, items in the news that are worth investigating, and personal

Most Important: Reflecting
- ➢ What went well?
- ➢ What could be adjusted?
- ➢ What to stop doing?
- ➢ What to start doing?
- ➢ What to continue doing?

You are welcome to use some of all of my Weekly Review, but the important thing is that you find what works best for you. Then place that Weekly Review Plan in your Personal Leadership Field Manual!

As you implement these principles, remember that productivity isn't about doing more things - it's about *doing the right things*. It's about creating the mental space to focus on high-impact activities that truly move the needle for your organization.

Reflection Questions:

1. *What's currently cluttering your mind? How could you capture these items in a trusted system outside your head?*
2. *Think about your current approach to processing emails or other inputs. How could applying the "Inbox Zero" concept improve your efficiency?*
3. *How might a regular Weekly Review change your leadership approach? What would you include in your review?*

Remember, mastering time management and productivity is a journey, not a destination. Start small, be patient with yourself, and focus on progress rather than perfection. As you develop these skills, you'll find yourself becoming a more focused, effective, and impactful leader.

Week 13 - Creativity and Idea Generation (James Webb Young)

"An idea is nothing more nor less than a new combination of old elements."

- James Webb Young

In our previous chapter, we explored the power of effective time management and productivity. Now, we turn our attention to another crucial leadership skill: creativity and idea generation. To guide us in this exploration, we'll draw on the wisdom of James Webb Young, an advertising executive who distilled the creative process into a practical, repeatable method.

In today's rapidly changing business landscape, creativity is no longer a luxury—*it's a necessity*. Leaders who can generate innovative solutions, inspire creative thinking in their teams, and navigate uncharted territories have a distinct advantage. But here's the good news: contrary to popular belief, creativity isn't just an innate talent. It's a skill that can be developed and honed with practice.

James Webb Young outlined a five-step process for creativity that we can apply in our leadership roles:

1. **Gather Raw Material:** This involves collecting information, both specific (related to the problem at hand) and general (a broad base of knowledge and experiences). As leaders, we should be constantly curious, reading widely, and exposing ourselves to diverse ideas and perspectives.

2. **Digest the Material:** In this stage, we examine the information we've gathered, looking at it from different angles and searching for connections. This might involve discussing ideas with others, sketching out concepts, or simply reflecting deeply on the problem.

3. **Unconscious Processing:** This is where we step away from the problem and let our subconscious mind work on it. It might involve engaging in unrelated activities, getting some rest, or focusing on other tasks.

4. **The "Eureka" Moment:** This is when the idea suddenly appears. It often happens when we least expect it—in the shower, during a walk, or just as we're falling asleep.

5. **Idea Meets Reality:** Finally, we bring our idea into the real world, refining and developing it. This is where we test its practicality and make necessary adjustments.

Applying this process in leadership can be transformative. When faced with a challenging problem, instead of immediately jumping to solutions, we can take a step back and engage in deliberate creative thinking. We can gather information from diverse sources, discuss the issue with our team, allow time for unconscious processing, and create an environment where "eureka" moments are encouraged and captured.

Practical Application:

Your Leadership Challenge: Clash of the Titans

Samantha is the newly promoted CEO of Titan Industries, a large manufacturing company. Upon taking the reins, she discovers that two of her most senior executives, the VP of Sales and the CFO, have a long-standing bitter rivalry. Their animosity is starting to create silos between their departments and negatively impact company culture.

The VP of Sales, Jack, is the company's top revenue driver but has a brash, cowboy attitude. Jack openly criticizes the CFO, Molly, for being too cautious and conservative with investments into new markets.

Molly, who has been with Titan Industries for 20 years, considers Jack to be reckless and short-sighted, putting quarterly numbers ahead of long-term stability. She constantly pushes back on his aggressive sales forecasts and budget requests.

Their feud has escalated since Samantha took charge, with each of them trying to persuade her to take their side. Meanwhile, their respective teams are becoming increasingly antagonistic, collaboration has ground to a halt, and the toxic environment is driving up turnover.

As CEO, Samantha knows she must address this executive team dysfunction before it does irreparable damage to the company. However, she is unsure of the best approach to take, especially as a new leader who needs to establish her authority and gain the trust of her C-suite.

What should Samantha do?

Follow through this process from James Webb Young and see where you end up based on the scenario outlined above:

- ☐ **5 minutes:** Gather information about the problem
- ☐ **3 minutes:** Reflect on and organize the information
- ☐ **2 minutes:** Take a brief mental break
- ☐ **5 minutes:** Brainstorm solutions

What solution(s) did you develop?

It is important to know that as leaders we have agency to foster creativity in our teams. Some great ways to ensure that happens is to:

- → Encouraging curiosity and continuous learning
- → Creating psychological safety where team members feel comfortable sharing unconventional ideas
- → Allowing time for reflection and unconscious processing
- → Celebrating creative thinking, even when ideas don't pan out
- → Modeling creative problem-solving in our own approach to challenges

Remember, creativity isn't just about coming up with wild, out-of-the-box ideas. It's about finding new connections between existing elements, seeing patterns where others see chaos, and imagining possibilities where others see dead ends. It's a crucial skill for navigating the complexities of modern leadership.

Reflection Questions:

1. *Think about a current challenge you're facing. How could you apply Young's five-step process to generate new solutions?*

2. *What sources could you tap into to gather more "raw material" for your creative thinking?*

3. *How can you create more space in your leadership role for unconscious processing and "eureka" moments?*

As you go through your week, look for opportunities to apply this creative process. Challenge yourself to approach problems with fresh eyes and an open mind. Remember, every great innovation started as a simple idea. By honing your creative skills, you're not just solving today's problems—you're preparing yourself and your team for the challenges of tomorrow.

Part 2:

Leadership and Team Building

Week 14 - Traits of Exceptional Leaders (John Maxwell)

"Leadership is not about titles, positions, or flowcharts.
It is about one life influencing another." - John Maxwell

In our previous chapter, we explored the power of creativity and idea generation in leadership. Now, in Part 2 of our journey into Leadership, we turn our attention to the core traits that define exceptional leaders. To guide us in this exploration, we'll draw on the wisdom of John Maxwell, a renowned leadership expert who has spent decades studying and teaching about effective leadership.

Maxwell argues that while leadership skills can be learned and developed, there are certain traits that set exceptional leaders apart. By understanding and cultivating these traits, we can significantly enhance our leadership effectiveness.

Let's explore some of the key traits Maxwell identifies:

1. **Influence:** At its core, leadership is about influence. Exceptional leaders have the ability to inspire and motivate others to action. They lead not just through authority, but through example, persuasion, and inspiration.

2. **Integrity:** Trust is the foundation of leadership, and integrity is the cornerstone of trust. Exceptional leaders are consistent in their words and actions, they keep their promises, and they stand by their values even when it's difficult.

3. **Self-Discipline:** Leadership often requires making tough decisions and persevering through challenges. Exceptional leaders have the self-discipline to stay focused on their goals, manage their time effectively, and consistently do what needs to be done.

4. **Vision:** Great leaders have a clear vision of where they want to go and the ability to communicate that vision in a way that inspires others. They can see possibilities where others see obstacles.

5. **Problem-Solving Skills:** Leadership inevitably involves facing challenges and solving problems. Exceptional leaders approach problems with creativity and determination, seeing them as opportunities for growth and innovation.

6. **Positive Attitude:** Optimism is contagious, and exceptional leaders maintain a positive attitude even in difficult circumstances. They focus on solutions rather than problems and inspire confidence in their teams.

7. **Continuous Learning:** The best leaders are lifelong learners. They're curious, open to new ideas, and always seeking to improve themselves and their leadership skills.

As we reflect on these traits, it's important to remember that no leader is perfect in all areas. The key is to honestly assess our strengths and areas for improvement, and to commit to ongoing growth and development.

Self-Assessment Break

★ On a scale of 1-10, how would you rate yourself on each of these traits?
- Influence: _____
- Integrity: _____
- Self-Discipline: _____
- Vision: _____
- Problem-Solving Skills: _____
- Positive Attitude: _____
- Continuous Learning: _____

★ Which trait do you consider your strongest?

★ Which one needs the most improvement?

Once you've identified an area for growth, create a specific plan for development. This might involve seeking out mentorship, reading books on the topic, taking a course, or simply practicing the trait in your daily leadership activities. Remember, small, consistent actions over time can lead to significant growth.

★ What skill are you focusing on, and what is your growth objective?

★ What is your plan on improving this area?

As leaders, we should also be attuned to these traits in others. How can we foster integrity, self-discipline, or problem-solving skills in our team members? How can we create an environment that encourages continuous learning and positive attitudes?

Reflection Questions:

1. *Think of a leader you admire. Which of Maxwell's traits do they exemplify? How do these traits contribute to their effectiveness?*

2. *Consider a recent leadership challenge you faced. How might strengthening one of these traits have helped you navigate the situation more effectively?*
   What's one specific action you can take this week to develop one of these leadership traits?

Remember, great leaders are not born, they're made through continuous effort and development. By focusing on cultivating these key traits, we can enhance our leadership effectiveness and make a greater positive impact on those we lead.

As you go through your week, pay attention to how these traits manifest in your leadership style. Look for opportunities to practice and strengthen them. And remember, leadership is a journey, not a destination. Each day presents new opportunities for growth and development as we strive to become the exceptional leaders our teams and organizations need.

Application Activity

Case Study: The Struggling Project Manager

Sarah, a senior manager at a software development company, has been observing one of her project managers, Alex, struggling with team leadership. Alex has been with the company for three years and has strong technical skills, but recently, his projects have been falling behind schedule, and team morale seems low.

Sarah has noticed the following issues:

❖ Alex often makes decisions without consulting team members, leading to resentment and missed opportunities for collaboration.
❖ When faced with obstacles, Alex tends to blame external factors rather than seeking creative solutions.
❖ Team members have reported feeling micromanaged and not trusted to complete their tasks independently.
❖ Alex rarely participates in professional development opportunities offered by the company.
❖ During team meetings, Alex's communication style is often perceived as abrupt and dismissive of others' ideas.

Sarah recognizes that Alex has potential but needs guidance to develop stronger leadership skills. She wants to approach this situation in a way that fosters growth and improvement rather than criticism.

Questions for Reflection and Discussion:

1. How can Sarah initiate a constructive conversation with Alex about his leadership challenges without making him feel accused or defensive?

2. What specific strategies could Sarah suggest to help Alex improve his integrity and build trust within his team?

3. What approaches could Sarah use to encourage Alex to engage in continuous learning and professional development?

4. What kind of environment or support system could Sarah create within the organization to promote the development of these positive traits (the seven listed above) in all team leaders?

5. How might Sarah use this situation as an opportunity to model effective coaching and mentorship for other managers in the company?

6. What metrics or indicators could Sarah use to measure improvement in Alex's leadership skills and team performance over time?

7. What potential barriers might Sarah encounter in her efforts to coach Alex, and how could she prepare to address them?

Week 15 - Servant Leadership (Robert Greenleaf)

"The servant-leader is servant first... It begins with the natural feeling that one wants to serve, to serve first." - Robert K. Greenleaf

In our previous chapter, we explored the traits of exceptional leaders as identified by John Maxwell. Now, we turn our attention to a powerful leadership philosophy that has gained significant traction in recent decades: servant leadership. This concept, introduced by Robert K. Greenleaf in 1970, turns traditional notions of leadership on their head.

At its core, servant leadership is about putting the needs of others first. It's a leadership approach that focuses on the growth and well-being of people and the communities to which they belong. Unlike traditional leadership models that often emphasize the power of the leader, servant leadership suggests that true leadership emerges from a desire to help others.

Let's explore some key principles of servant leadership:

1. **Putting Others' Needs First:** Servant leaders prioritize the needs of their team members over their own. They ask, "How can I help?" rather than "How can I be served?"

2. **Empowering and Developing People:** Servant leaders focus on the growth and development of their team members. They provide opportunities for learning and advancement, and they celebrate others' successes.

3. **Humility and Authenticity:** Servant leaders lead with humility. They admit when they're wrong, they're open to feedback, and they don't let ego drive their decisions.

4. **Building Community:** Servant leaders foster a sense of community within their organizations. They encourage collaboration, promote inclusivity, and work to create a positive organizational culture.

5. **Listening and Empathy:** Servant leaders are attentive listeners. They seek to understand others' perspectives and experiences, showing genuine care and empathy.

6. **Foresight and Stewardship:** While focused on serving others, servant leaders also maintain a long-term perspective. They make decisions with an eye toward the future and the greater good.

Adopting a servant leadership approach can have profound effects on an organization. It can lead to increased employee engagement, higher job satisfaction, improved team performance, and a more positive work environment. When people feel valued, supported, and empowered, they're more likely to give their best effort and to stay committed to the organization.

Story Time

In his seminal essay "The Servant as Leader," Greenleaf shares the story of Leo from Hermann Hesse's novel *Journey to the East*. In the story, Leo is a servant who accompanies a group of travelers on a mythical journey. He does menial chores for the group but also sustains them with his spirit and song. Leo is cheerful, caring, and attentive to everyone's needs.

When Leo disappears, the group falls into disarray and the journey is abandoned. Years later, the narrator discovers that Leo, who he had known as a servant, was actually the titular head of the Order that had sponsored the journey. Leo was a leader all along, but his leadership was expressed through service.

Greenleaf uses this story to illustrate that the most effective leaders are those who lead by serving others. Leo's humble service had been the glue holding the group together, demonstrating that true leadership is not about power or position, but about meeting the needs of others and helping them grow.

Application Questions:

1. Think about a time in your career when you encountered a leader who embodied the servant-first approach like Leo. How did their leadership style impact the team's morale, productivity, and overall success?

2. In your current leadership role, what is one specific way you could emulate Leo's approach? How might prioritizing service to your team members enhance your effectiveness as a leader?

However, servant leadership isn't without its challenges. It requires a fundamental shift in mindset for many leaders. It can be time-consuming, as it often involves more listening, more collaboration, and more focus on individual team members' needs. It also requires vulnerability and the willingness to admit that you don't have all the answers.

As you consider incorporating servant leadership into your own practice, reflect on these questions:

1. In what ways do you currently put the needs of your team members first? Where could you improve in this area?

2. How do you actively contribute to the growth and development of those you lead?

3. Are there areas where your ego might be getting in the way of truly serving your team?

4. How could you create more opportunities for listening and understanding in your leadership role?

Remember, becoming a servant leader is a journey, not a destination. It's about consistently striving to serve others and to create an environment where people can thrive. Start small - perhaps by focusing on one principle of servant leadership this week. Pay attention to how it affects your interactions with your team and the overall dynamics of your workplace.

As you go through your week, look for opportunities to put others first, to listen more deeply, to empower and develop your team members. Notice how this shift in focus impacts your leadership effectiveness and your team's performance. You may find that by focusing less on being "the leader" and more on serving others, you become an even more influential and impactful leader.

Reflection Questions:

1. *Think of a time when you experienced servant leadership from someone else. How did it impact you? What can you learn from that experience?*

2. *What's one specific way you could incorporate more servant leadership into your practice this week?*

3. *How might adopting a servant leadership approach change the culture of your team or organization?*

By embracing servant leadership, we have the opportunity to not just lead more effectively, but to make a profound positive impact on the lives of those we lead and the organizations we serve. It's a powerful reminder that true leadership is not about us - it's about those we have the privilege to serve and support.

Personal Development

Grab your Personal Leadership Field Manual (PLFM) and a sheet of paper:

★ On your paper, write Servant Leadership at the top of the page.

★ Then define Servant Leadership in your own Words.

★ The write these questions and answer them:
   ○ How am I currently incorporating servant leadership principles?
   ○ In what areas could I be more of a servant leader?
   ○ What are potential obstacles to adopting a servant leadership approach?

★ Finally, pick your first actionable step on adopting more Servant Leadership, maybe it is listening to clients more completely, maybe it is being more humble, whatever it is - set your first step!

Week 16 - Emotional Intelligence (Daniel Goleman)

"In a very real sense we have two minds,
one that thinks and one that feels." - Daniel Goleman

In our previous chapter, we explored the transformative power of servant leadership. Now, we turn our attention to another crucial aspect of leadership effectiveness: emotional intelligence (EI). Popularized by psychologist Daniel Goleman, emotional intelligence refers to the ability to recognize, understand, and manage our own emotions, as well as the emotions of others.

Goleman argues that EI is often more important than IQ in determining leadership success. While technical skills and cognitive abilities are certainly important, it's our emotional intelligence that truly sets great leaders apart. Leaders with high EI are better able to navigate complex interpersonal dynamics, inspire and motivate their teams, and create positive work environments.

Let's explore the five key components of emotional intelligence:

1. **Self-awareness:** This is the foundation of EI. It involves recognizing our own emotions, understanding our strengths and weaknesses, and having a strong sense of self-worth. Self-aware leaders can accurately assess their own performance and understand how their emotions impact others.

2. **Self-regulation:** This involves managing our emotions, especially in stressful or challenging situations. Leaders with strong self-regulation can stay calm under pressure, think before acting, and adapt to changing circumstances.

3. **Motivation:** This refers to our inner drive to achieve, improve, and meet our goals. Highly motivated leaders are passionate about their work, optimistic in the face of setbacks, and committed to their organization's success.

4. **Empathy:** This is the ability to understand and share the feelings of others. Empathetic leaders can sense the emotional climate of their team, understand different perspectives, and respond appropriately to others' concerns.

5. **Social skills:** This encompasses a range of interpersonal skills, including communication, conflict resolution, and the ability to build and maintain relationships. Leaders with strong social skills are effective communicators, team builders, and change catalysts.

Developing Emotional Intelligence

The good news is that emotional intelligence can be developed and improved over time. Here are some strategies for enhancing each component of EI:

Self-awareness:
- Practice mindfulness meditation
- Keep a journal to reflect on your emotions and reactions
- Seek feedback from others on your behavior and impact

Self-regulation:
- Practice stress-management techniques like deep breathing or progressive muscle relaxation
- Pause before responding in emotional situations
- Identify your emotional triggers and develop strategies to manage them

Motivation:
- Set challenging but achievable goals for yourself
- Cultivate a growth mindset
- Find ways to connect your work to your personal values and passions

Empathy:
- Practice active listening
- Put yourself in others' shoes
- Pay attention to non-verbal cues in interactions

Social skills:
- Practice clear and assertive communication
- Seek out opportunities for collaboration
- Work on your conflict resolution skills

EI Self-Assessment

Take a moment to rate yourself on each of the five components of emotional intelligence on a scale of 1-10, with 1 being very low and 10 being very high. Be honest with yourself - this is for your own growth and development.

Self-awareness: ___
Self-regulation: ___
Motivation: ___
Empathy: ___
Social skills: ___

Reflect on your scores.

★ Which area is your strongest?

★ Which area needs the most improvement?

★ How do these scores align with your experiences as a leader?

Applying Emotional Intelligence in Leadership

As you go through your week, look for opportunities to practice and develop your emotional intelligence. Here are some ideas:

➢ Before important meetings or decisions, take a moment to check in with your own emotions. How are you feeling? How might these feelings impact your behavior or decisions?

➢ When interacting with team members, practice active listening. Try to understand not just the content of what they're saying, but the emotions behind it.

➤ When faced with a challenging situation, pause before responding. Take a deep breath and consider how you can respond in a way that's both authentic to your feelings and constructive for the situation.

➤ At the end of each day, reflect on your interactions. Where did you demonstrate emotional intelligence? Where could you have done better?

Remember, developing emotional intelligence is a journey, not a destination. It requires ongoing self-reflection, practice, and a willingness to learn from both successes and mistakes. But the payoff - *in terms of leadership effectiveness, team performance, and personal satisfaction* - is immense.

As Daniel Goleman says, "If your emotional abilities aren't in hand, if you don't have self-awareness, if you are not able to manage your distressing emotions, if you can't have empathy and have effective relationships, then no matter how smart you are, you are not going to get very far."

By cultivating emotional intelligence, we not only become more effective leaders, but we also create more positive, productive, and fulfilling work environments for ourselves and those we lead.

Reflection Questions:

1. *Think of a recent leadership challenge you faced. How could stronger emotional intelligence have helped you navigate that situation more effectively?*

2. *What's one specific action you can take this week to develop your weakest area of emotional intelligence?*

3. *How can you create opportunities for your team members to develop their own emotional intelligence?*

As we continue our leadership journey, let's remember that true leadership isn't just about what we know or what we can do - it's about how we connect with, understand, and inspire others. And that's where emotional intelligence truly shines.

EI in Action - Case Study

Sarah, a team leader at a Maple Syrup startup, is facing a challenging situation. Her team is behind on an important project deadline, and tensions are running high. During a team meeting, two of her team members get into a heated argument about the best approach to catch up. Other team members are visibly uncomfortable, and the meeting is quickly derailing.

Questions:

1. How could Sarah use self-awareness and self-regulation in this situation?

2. How might empathy help Sarah navigate this conflict?

3. What social skills could Sarah employ to get the meeting back on track?

4. How could Sarah use this situation as an opportunity to motivate her team?

Week 17 - Communication Skills (Dale Carnegie)

"You can make more friends in two months by becoming interested in other people than you can in two years by trying to get other people interested in you." - Dale Carnegie

In our previous chapter, we explored the crucial role of emotional intelligence in leadership. Now, we turn our attention to another fundamental leadership skill: *effective communication*. To guide us in this exploration, we'll draw on the timeless wisdom of Dale Carnegie, whose book *How to Win Friends and Influence People* has been inspiring leaders for nearly a century.

Carnegie's approach to communication is rooted in a simple yet profound idea: to be an effective communicator, you must first be genuinely interested in others. This principle aligns closely with the servant leadership and emotional intelligence concepts we've explored in previous chapters, emphasizing the importance of empathy and human connection in leadership.

Let's delve into some of Carnegie's key principles for effective communication:

1. **Become genuinely interested in other people:** Carnegie argues that the best way to get someone's attention is to show sincere interest in them. As leaders, this means taking the time to understand our team members' perspectives, goals, and challenges.

2. **Be a good listener and encourage others to talk about themselves:** Effective communication isn't just about what we say - it's also about how well we listen. By giving others the space to express themselves, we not only gain valuable insights but also build trust and rapport.

3. **Make the other person feel important - and do it sincerely:** Everyone wants to feel valued and appreciated. As leaders, we can boost morale and motivation by sincerely acknowledging the contributions and worth of each team member.

4. **Avoid criticism, condemnation, and complaint:** Carnegie emphasizes the importance of positive communication. While constructive feedback is necessary, constant criticism can be demoralizing and counterproductive.

5. **Give honest and sincere appreciation:** Recognizing and appreciating others' efforts and achievements is a powerful motivator. Carnegie stresses that this appreciation must be genuine to be effective.

These principles might seem simple, but their consistent application can transform our leadership communication. Let's explore how we can put these ideas into practice.

Active Listening Exercise:

Find a partner and take turns sharing a work-related challenge for 2 minutes each. As the listener, practice these active listening techniques:

- Maintain eye contact
- Use non-verbal cues (nodding, leaning in) to show engagement
- Avoid interrupting
- Ask clarifying questions
- Summarize what you've heard to ensure understanding

After both partners have shared, discuss:

1. How did it feel to be truly listened to?

2. What challenges did you face in listening actively?

3. How could this approach improve communication in your leadership role?

Developing Your Communication Skills

Improving our communication skills is an ongoing process. Here are some strategies to help you continue developing:

→ **Practice empathetic listening:** Make a conscious effort to listen not just to the words, but to the emotions and intentions behind them.

→ **Use "you" language:** Frame your communication from the listener's perspective. Instead of "I think this project is important," try "This project could really benefit your team."

→ **Be aware of non-verbal communication:** Your body language, tone of voice, and facial expressions all communicate messages. Ensure they align with your words.

→ **Seek feedback:** Regularly ask for feedback on your communication style. What's working well? Where could you improve?

→ **Tailor your communication:** Different people respond to different communication styles. Learn to adapt your approach based on your audience.

As you go through your week, look for opportunities to apply Carnegie's principles. Pay attention to how people respond when you show genuine interest, when you listen actively, when you offer sincere appreciation. Notice how these small changes in your communication style can have a big impact on your leadership effectiveness.

Case Study: The Power of Genuine Interest

When Emily Chen took over as regional manager for a growing IT services firm, she quickly realized that one of her teams was struggling. Deadlines were being missed, communication felt tense, and turnover was creeping up.

Instead of jumping straight into performance reviews or new policies, Emily spent her first few weeks simply meeting with each team member one-on-one. Her only goal: to listen. She asked questions like, "What do you enjoy most about your work?" and "What's one thing you'd change if you could?" She took notes, followed up on personal details, and made sure to remember what mattered most to each person.

Within a month, something shifted. The team began bringing up ideas unprompted, problem-solving sessions became more relaxed, and collaboration increased. One senior developer told her privately, "It's been a while since anyone asked what I thought about how we work. It actually makes me want to go the extra mile again."

Emily didn't use motivational speeches or financial rewards — she built trust by showing genuine interest. Her active listening created psychological safety, and in turn, her team became far more engaged and productive.

Application Questions:

1. How did Emily's approach align with Carnegie's principle of showing genuine interest in others?

2. What impact did her listening have on trust, engagement, and team performance?

3. How could you incorporate regular, genuine interest in your own leadership practice? For example, how might you create a culture of listening within your team?

Remember, as Carnegie said, "There is only one way... to get anybody to do anything. And that is by making the other person want to do it." By mastering the art of communication, we can inspire, motivate, and lead more effectively, creating positive change in our teams and organizations.

Reflection Questions:

1. *Think of a leader you admire for their communication skills. How do they embody Carnegie's principles?*

2. *What's one specific way you could show more genuine interest in your team members this week?*

3. *How might improving your communication skills enhance your overall leadership effectiveness?*

As we continue our leadership journey, let's remember that effective communication is not just about transmitting information - it's about connecting with others, understanding their perspectives, and inspiring them to achieve their best. By honing our communication skills, we can become the kind of leaders who not only get things done but who also bring out the best in those around us.

The Appreciation Challenge:

For the next week, challenge yourself to give sincere appreciation to at least one person each day. This could be a team member, a colleague, or even someone outside of work. Keep a journal of these interactions, noting:

- Who you appreciated and for what

- How you expressed your appreciation

- The person's reaction

- How the interaction made you feel

At the end of the week, reflect on how this practice impacted your relationships and leadership approach.

Week 18 - Building Trust and Psychological Safety (Patrick Lencioni)

"Trust is the foundation of real teamwork." - Patrick Lencioni

In our previous chapter, we explored the art of communication through the lens of Dale Carnegie's timeless wisdom. Now, we turn our attention to another critical aspect of leadership: building trust and psychological safety within teams. To guide us in this exploration, we'll draw on the insights of Patrick Lencioni, renowned author and organizational health expert.

Lencioni's work, particularly his book *The Five Dysfunctions of a Team*, emphasizes that trust is the bedrock upon which all effective teamwork is built. Without trust, teams struggle to engage in productive conflict, commit to decisions, hold each other accountable, or achieve collective results.

But what exactly do we mean by trust in a professional context? Lencioni describes it as "vulnerability-based trust." This goes beyond simply believing that your teammates will do their jobs competently. It's about team members feeling safe to be open about their weaknesses, mistakes, fears, and behaviors. It's about creating an environment where people can be genuinely vulnerable with one another.

Closely related to trust is the concept of psychological safety, a term popularized by Harvard Business School professor Amy Edmondson. Psychological safety refers to a shared belief that the team is safe for interpersonal risk-taking. In psychologically safe teams, members feel they can speak up, share ideas, and make mistakes without fear of negative consequences to their self-image, status, or career.

Personal History Exercise:

Lencioni suggests this exercise as a way to build vulnerability-based trust:

In a team meeting, have each person share three things about their personal history:
- Where they grew up
- How many siblings they have and where they fall in the birth order
- The most significant challenge of their childhood

After everyone has shared, discuss:

- What did you learn about your teammates that you didn't know before?
- How does knowing these personal details change your perception of your teammates?
- How might this kind of sharing contribute to building trust?

Let's explore some key strategies for building trust and psychological safety:

1. **Lead by example**: As a leader, you set the tone for vulnerability. Share your own weaknesses and mistakes. Admit when you don't have all the answers.

2. **Encourage open dialogue:** Create opportunities for team members to share their thoughts, concerns, and ideas freely.

3. **Respond positively to vulnerability:** When team members do open up, respond with empathy and support, not judgment.

4. **Foster personal connections:** Encourage team members to get to know each other as individuals, not just as colleagues.

5. **Address conflicts constructively:** Don't let tensions simmer beneath the surface. Address conflicts openly and constructively.

6. **Celebrate failures as learning opportunities:** Reframe failures as chances to learn and grow, not as reasons for punishment or shame.

Case Study: The Power of Psychological Safety at Google

In 2012, Google embarked on a quest to build the perfect team. Their research initiative, Project Aristotle, studied hundreds of Google's teams to determine why some stumbled while others soared. The researchers found that the most important factor in team effectiveness was psychological safety.

One example they cited involved two teams:

Team A was filled with top executives, each graduating from elite universities and renowned for their individual accomplishments. However, when they worked together, they struggled. Team members would interrupt each other, compete for leadership, and subtly undermine each other.

Team B, on the other hand, was a mix of generalists, with no particularly impressive individual accomplishments. Yet, they worked together seamlessly. They listened to each other, showed sensitivity to each other's moods, and created a safe space for taking risks.

The key difference? *Psychological safety.*
In Team B, members felt safe to take risks, voice their opinions, and be vulnerable in front of each other. This allowed them to harness their collective intelligence and outperform the ostensibly "stronger" Team A.

Questions for reflection:
- How does this case study illustrate the importance of trust and psychological safety?

- Can you think of examples from your own experience where a lack of psychological safety hindered team performance?

- What specific actions could you take as a leader to foster greater psychological safety in your team?

Developing Trust and Psychological Safety

Building trust and psychological safety is an ongoing process. Here are some strategies to help you continue developing these crucial elements:

1. **Practice active listening:** Show that you value your team members' input by listening attentively and responding thoughtfully.

2. **Be consistent:** Align your words and actions. Consistency builds predictability, which is crucial for trust.

3. **Show competence:** While vulnerability is important, it's also crucial that your team trusts in your ability to lead. Continuously develop your skills and knowledge.

4. **Be transparent:** Share information openly. When you can't share something, explain why.

5. **Follow through on commitments:** Do what you say you'll do. If circumstances change, communicate proactively.

As you go through your week, look for opportunities to build trust and psychological safety. Pay attention to how team members respond when you show vulnerability, when you encourage open dialogue, when you celebrate learning from failures. Notice how these practices impact team dynamics and performance.

Remember, as Lencioni says, "Teamwork begins by building trust. And the only way to do that is to overcome our need for invulnerability." By fostering trust and psychological safety, we create an environment where team members can bring their whole selves to work, take risks, innovate, and achieve extraordinary results together.

Reflection Questions:

1. *Think of a time when you felt a high level of trust and psychological safety in a team. What did the leader do to create that environment?*

2. *What's one specific way you could demonstrate vulnerability with your team this week?*

3. *How might improving trust and psychological safety in your team enhance overall performance and job satisfaction?*

As we continue our leadership journey, let's remember that building trust and psychological safety is not a one-time event, but an ongoing commitment. It requires courage, consistency, and genuine care for our team members. By prioritizing these elements, we can create teams that are not just high-performing, but also deeply fulfilling to be part of.

Trust Behaviors Self-Assessment:

Rate yourself on a scale of 1 (rarely) to 5 (almost always) on the following trust-building behaviors:

___ I admit my mistakes openly
___ I ask for help when I need it
___ I accept questions and input about my area of responsibility
___ I give others the benefit of the doubt before arriving at a negative conclusion
___ I take risks in offering feedback and assistance to others
___ I focus on desired results rather than protecting my position

Reflect on your scores.
Which areas are your strengths?
Where could you improve?
What specific actions could you take to enhance your trust-building behaviors?

Week 19 - Giving Feedback and Performance Reviews

"Feedback is the breakfast of champions." - Ken Blanchard

In our previous chapter, we explored the crucial role of trust and psychological safety in building effective teams. Now, we turn our attention to a leadership skill that both requires and reinforces that foundation of trust: giving feedback and conducting performance reviews.

Effective feedback is a cornerstone of leadership. It's how we guide, develop, and motivate our team members. When done well, feedback can inspire growth, boost performance, and strengthen relationships. When done poorly, it can demoralize, confuse, and create resentment. As leaders, mastering the art of feedback is essential for our success and the success of our teams.

Let's start by exploring the key principles of effective feedback:

1. **Be specific and behavior-focused:** Vague feedback like "good job" or "you need to improve" is rarely helpful. Instead, focus on specific behaviors and their impacts. For example, "Your detailed analysis in the quarterly report helped us identify key areas for improvement."

2. **Balance positive and constructive feedback:** While it's important to address areas for improvement, don't forget to recognize and reinforce positive behaviors. Aim for a ratio of about 3:1 positive to constructive feedback.

3. **Be timely:** Feedback is most effective when given close to the event or behavior in question. Don't wait for formal reviews to provide important feedback.

4. **Make it a two-way conversation:** Effective feedback is a dialogue, not a monologue. Encourage the recipient to share their perspective and collaborate on solutions.

5. **Follow up and support improvement:** Feedback shouldn't be a one-time event. Follow up to check on progress and provide support for improvement.

Video Time:

To see these principles in action, let's watch a brief video from Harvard Business Review on How to Give Constructive Feedback (5 min)

[https://www.youtube.com/watch?v=wtl5UrrgU8c]

As you watch, consider:
- How does the video exemplify the principles we've discussed?
- What new insights does it offer about giving effective feedback?

Feedback Role-Play:

Find a partner and take turns practicing giving feedback using the following scenarios:

Scenario 1: A team member has been consistently late to meetings, causing delays and frustration among the team.

Scenario 2: A team member went above and beyond to help a colleague complete a crucial project on time.

After each role-play, discuss:
- How well did the feedback align with the principles of effective feedback?
- How did it feel to give/receive the feedback?
- What could be improved in the feedback delivery?

Now, let's turn our attention to a more formal feedback process: the performance review. While regular, informal feedback should be ongoing, performance reviews provide a structured opportunity to discuss overall performance, set goals, and plan for development.

Here are some best practices for conducting effective performance reviews:

1. Prepare thoroughly: Review the employee's job description, previous goals, and performance data. Gather input from others who work closely with the employee.

2. Create a comfortable environment: Choose a private location and allow enough time for a thorough discussion without interruptions.

3. <u>Focus on facts and specific behaviors</u>: Use concrete examples to illustrate your points, avoiding generalizations or personal judgments.

4. <u>Set clear goals and expectations</u>: Collaborate with the employee to set SMART (Specific, Measurable, Achievable, Relevant, Time-bound) goals for the coming period.

5. <u>End on a positive note</u>: Conclude the review by expressing confidence in the employee's ability to meet their goals and reiterating your support for their development.

How to present like a champ from the start:

To help us think about how to start a performance review effectively, let's watch a video on presentation openers. While it's about presentations, many of the principles apply to opening a performance review:

<u>How to Do a Presentation - 5 Steps to a Killer Opener</u> (7 min)
[https://www.youtube.com/watch?v=dEDcc0aCjaA]

As you watch, consider:
- How could these opening techniques be adapted for a performance review?
- Which technique do you think would be most effective in putting an employee at ease at the start of a review?

Developing Your Feedback Skills

Improving our ability to give feedback and conduct performance reviews is an ongoing process. Here are some strategies to help you continue developing these crucial skills:

1. **Seek feedback on your feedback**: Ask team members how your feedback could be more helpful to them.

2. **Practice regularly**: Don't wait for formal reviews to give feedback. Look for opportunities to provide feedback in your day-to-day interactions.

3. **Reflect on your own experiences**: Think about the best and worst feedback you've received. What made it effective or ineffective?

4. **Role-play challenging conversations**: Practice difficult feedback conversations with a trusted colleague or mentor.

5. **Stay updated on best practices**: Regularly read articles or attend workshops on effective feedback and performance management.

As you go through your week, look for opportunities to provide both positive and constructive feedback to your team members. Pay attention to their reactions and the impact of your feedback. Notice how regular, effective feedback can improve performance and strengthen your relationships with your team.

Remember, as Ken Blanchard says, "Feedback is the breakfast of champions." By mastering the art of giving feedback and conducting performance reviews, we can nourish our team's growth, fuel their performance, and cultivate a culture of continuous improvement.

Reflection Questions:

1. *Think of the best feedback you've ever received. What made it so effective? How can you incorporate those elements into your own feedback style?*

2. *What's one specific way you could improve your approach to performance reviews?*

3. *How might improving your feedback skills enhance your overall leadership effectiveness and team performance?*

As we continue our leadership journey, let's commit to making feedback a regular, constructive part of our leadership practice. By doing so, we can help our team members reach their full potential and create a culture of growth and excellence in our organizations.

Week 20 - Conflict Resolution (Thomas-Kilmann)

"The quality of our lives depends not on whether or not we have conflicts, but on how we respond to them." - Thomas Crum

In our previous chapter, we explored the art of giving feedback and conducting performance reviews. Now, we turn our attention to two critical leadership skills that often go hand in hand: conflict resolution and negotiation. As leaders, our ability to navigate conflicts and negotiate effectively can make the difference between a thriving, collaborative team and one mired in tension and inefficiency.

Conflict is an inevitable part of human interaction, especially in the workplace where diverse perspectives, competing priorities, and high-stakes decisions are commonplace. However, conflict isn't inherently negative. When handled skillfully, it can lead to innovation, stronger relationships, and better outcomes. The key lies in how we approach and manage these conflicts.

Let's start by exploring some key principles of effective conflict resolution:

1. **Active Listening:** This involves fully concentrating on what is being said rather than just passively hearing the words. It means listening with all senses and giving full attention to the speaker. In conflict situations, active listening can help uncover underlying issues and show respect for all parties involved.
2. **Empathy and Perspective-Taking:** Try to understand the situation from the other person's point of view. This doesn't mean you have to agree with them, but understanding their perspective can lead to more constructive dialogue and solutions.
3. **Focus on Interests, Not Positions:** Often in conflicts, people take hard positions ("I must have X"). Instead, try to uncover the underlying interests ("I need X because..."). This approach opens up more possibilities for resolution.
4. **Generate Win-Win Solutions:** Aim for outcomes where all parties feel their needs have been addressed to some degree. This promotes long-term resolution and strengthens relationships.

Exercise 1: Conflict Resolution Role-Play

Find a partner and role-play the following scenario:

Two team members disagree on the approach to a major project. One wants to use a tried-and-true method, while the other wants to try a new, potentially more efficient but riskier approach. As the leader, your task is to help resolve this conflict.

After the role-play, discuss:

- How well were the principles of conflict resolution applied?
- What was challenging about the process?
- What strategies were most effective?

Now, let's turn our attention to negotiation skills. While often associated with formal business deals, negotiation is a daily part of leadership, whether we're allocating resources, setting project timelines, or managing team dynamics.

Here are some key strategies for effective negotiation:

1. **Preparation and Research:** Understand the issue from all angles. Know your priorities, the other party's likely priorities, and potential areas of common ground.

2. **Set Clear Objectives:** Know what you want to achieve, but also be clear about your minimum acceptable outcome.

3. **Build Rapport:** Establish a positive relationship with the other party. This can make the negotiation process smoother and more productive.

4. **Find Common Ground:** Look for shared interests or goals. These can be the foundation for mutually beneficial solutions.

5. **Be Willing to Compromise:** The best negotiations often involve give and take from both sides.

Exercise 2: Negotiation Scenario

Imagine you're negotiating with your boss for resources for a new project. You believe this project could significantly benefit the company, but resources are tight.

Take a few minutes to prepare your negotiation strategy:

- What are your key objectives?
- What research would you need to do?
- How could you frame this as a win-win proposition?
- What compromises might you be willing to make?

Share your strategy with a partner and discuss potential approaches and challenges.

Developing Your Conflict Resolution and Negotiation Skills

Improving these skills is an ongoing process. Here are some strategies to help you continue developing:

1. **Practice Active Listening:** In your daily interactions, focus on truly understanding others before responding.

2. **Seek Win-Win Solutions:** When conflicts arise, challenge yourself to find outcomes that benefit all parties.

3. **Role-Play Difficult Conversations:** Practice handling conflicts and negotiations with a trusted colleague or mentor.

4. **Learn from Each Experience:** After each conflict or negotiation, reflect on what went well and what you could improve.

5. **Study Successful Negotiators:** Read books or watch videos about effective negotiation techniques and try to incorporate these strategies into your own approach.

As you go through your week, pay attention to conflicts and negotiations in your workplace. How are they being handled? What could be improved? Look for opportunities to apply the principles we've discussed.

Remember, as Nelson Mandela said, "The greatest glory in living lies not in never falling, but in rising every time we fall." In the same way, our greatest achievements in conflict resolution and negotiation often come not from avoiding difficult situations, but from navigating them skillfully and emerging with stronger relationships and better outcomes.

Reflection Questions:

1. *Think of a recent conflict you encountered. How could you have applied these conflict resolution principles more effectively?*
2. *What's one specific way you could improve your negotiation skills this week?*
3. *How might enhancing your conflict resolution and negotiation skills impact your leadership effectiveness and team dynamics?*

As we continue our leadership journey, let's embrace conflicts and negotiations as opportunities for growth, collaboration, and positive change. By mastering these skills, we can create more harmonious, productive, and innovative work environments.

Week 21 - Motivate and Inspire (Zig Ziglar)

"You don't have to be great to start, but you have to start to be great." - Zig Ziglar

In our previous chapter, we explored the crucial skills of conflict resolution and negotiation. Now, we turn our attention to another vital aspect of leadership: the ability to motivate and inspire. To guide us in this exploration, we'll draw on the wisdom of one of the most influential motivational speakers of all time, Zig Ziglar.

Ziglar's approach to motivation is rooted in positivity, goal-setting, and service to others. His teachings have inspired millions of people worldwide, including countless leaders across various industries. Let's delve into some of Ziglar's key principles and explore how we can apply them in our leadership roles.

Video Break: Setting Goals | Zig Ziglar (5 min)
[https://www.youtube.com/watch?v=Ae-VJ_lauCw]

To start, let's watch one of Ziglar's most impactful talks on staying motivated:

As you watch, consider:

- What key messages resonate with you?
- How can these principles be applied in a leadership context?
- How do Ziglar's ideas align with or challenge your current approach to motivation?

Now, let's explore some of Ziglar's core principles for motivation and inspiration:

1. **Setting Clear Goals:** Ziglar often said, "If you aim at nothing, you will hit it every time." As leaders, we need to set clear, compelling goals for ourselves and our teams. These goals should be specific, measurable, achievable, relevant, and time-bound (SMART).
2. **Maintaining a Positive Attitude:** Ziglar was a firm believer in the power of positivity. He argued that our attitude, more than our aptitude, determines our altitude. As leaders, our attitude sets the tone for our entire team.
3. **Continuous Learning:** "There is no elevator to success. You have to take the stairs," Ziglar often said. This emphasizes the importance of continuous learning and growth.

As leaders, we should model this commitment to learning and create opportunities for our team members to develop their skills.

4. **The Power of Self-Talk:** Ziglar stressed the importance of positive self-talk and affirmations. He believed that the way we talk to ourselves significantly impacts our performance and outlook.

5. **Serving Others:** One of Ziglar's most famous quotes is, "You can have everything in life you want, if you will just help other people get what they want." This principle of service is crucial for inspirational leadership.

Exercise 1: Personal Motivation Plan

Take a few minutes to write down:

- Your top 3 professional goals for the next year
- 5 positive affirmations related to these goals
- 3 actions you can take this week to move towards these goals

Share your plan with a partner. Discuss how you can hold each other accountable and support each other's growth.

Exercise 2: Motivating Your Team

Think about a current challenge your team is facing. How can you apply Ziglar's principles to motivate and inspire your team through this challenge? Consider:

- How can you frame this challenge in a positive light?
- What clear, compelling goal can you set related to this challenge?
- How can you serve your team members in working towards this goal?

Write down your ideas and share them with a partner. Provide feedback to each other on your approaches.

Creating a Culture of Motivation and Inspiration

As leaders, our role goes beyond personal motivation - we need to create an environment where our entire team feels motivated and inspired. Here are some strategies to foster such a culture:

1. **Communicate a Clear Vision:** Help your team understand the bigger picture and how their work contributes to it.
2. **Recognize and Celebrate Achievements:** Regularly acknowledge both individual and team accomplishments.
3. **Provide Growth Opportunities:** Offer training, mentoring, and challenging assignments to help team members develop their skills.
4. **Lead by Example:** Demonstrate the attitude and work ethic you want to see in your team.
5. **Foster a Positive Environment:** Encourage positivity, teamwork, and mutual support among team members.

As you go through your week, look for opportunities to apply these motivational principles. Pay attention to how your words and actions impact your team's energy and engagement. Notice how a shift in your own attitude can ripple out to affect your entire team.

Remember, as Ziglar said, "People often say that motivation doesn't last. Well, neither does bathing - that's why we recommend it daily." Motivation and inspiration aren't one-time events, but ongoing practices that we need to cultivate consistently.

Reflection Questions:

1. *Think of a time when you felt highly motivated at work. What factors contributed to that motivation? How can you recreate those conditions for your team?*

2. *What's one specific way you could incorporate more positive self-talk into your daily routine?*

3. *How might improving your ability to motivate and inspire enhance your overall leadership effectiveness and team performance?*

As we continue our leadership journey, let's commit to being not just managers, but true motivators and inspirers. By embodying Ziglar's principles of positivity, goal-setting, continuous learning, and service to others, we can create teams that are not just productive, but truly energized and passionate about their work.

Week 22 - Hiring A-Players (Geoff Smart)

"The best leaders are the best recruiters." - Geoff Smart

In our previous chapter, we explored the art of motivation and inspiration. Now, we turn our attention to a critical aspect of leadership that can make or break an organization: hiring. Specifically, we'll focus on hiring A-Players, drawing on the wisdom of Geoff Smart, co-author of the influential book *Who: The A Method for Hiring*.

Smart argues that the single biggest lever for improving organizational performance is in who you hire. A-Players, as defined by Smart, are the top 10% of talent available for a given job, for a given compensation rate, in a given geographic area. These are the people who consistently deliver exceptional results and drive organizations forward.

But how do we identify and attract these A-Players? Smart proposes a method he calls the "Who" method, consisting of four key steps:

1. **Scorecard:** Before you start hiring, clearly define what you're hiring for. A scorecard is not a job description; it's a set of outcomes and competencies that define success in the role.
2. **Source:** Generate a flow of high-quality candidates. This involves systematic networking and referrals, not just posting job ads.
3. **Select:** Use a structured interview process to accurately assess candidates. This is where the "Who" interview comes in.
4. **Sell:** Once you've identified your A-Player, you need to persuade them to join your team.

Let's dive deeper into each of these steps.

The Scorecard

A good scorecard includes:

- The mission for the role
- Outcomes that define success (usually 3-8 specific, measurable results)
- Competencies required (both technical skills and cultural fit)

Exercise:

Create a scorecard for a key position in your organization.

- What are the critical outcomes this role needs to deliver?
- What competencies are essential for success?

Sourcing

Sourcing Smart emphasizes the importance of proactive sourcing. A-Players are often not actively job hunting. Strategies include:

- Systematic networking
- Employee referrals
- Maintaining relationships with potential future hires

Select

The "Who" Interview This structured interview process consists of:

1. **Career History Questions:** Walk through each job chronologically, asking about successes, mistakes, key decisions, and relationships.
2. **Focused Questions:** Probe for specific examples related to the outcomes and competencies in your scorecard.
3. **Situational Questions:** Present scenarios relevant to the role and ask how the candidate would handle them.

Selling

Once you've identified your A-Player, you need to persuade them to join. This involves:

- Understanding their motivations and career goals
- Clearly articulating the opportunity and how it aligns with their aspirations
- Addressing any concerns or obstacles

Smart's approach is data-driven and systematic, designed to remove much of the subjectivity and bias that often creeps into hiring decisions. By following this method, organizations can dramatically improve their hiring success rate and, consequently, their overall performance.

Case Study: The "Who" Method

Consider the case of a tech startup that implemented the "Who" method. They were hiring for a crucial VP of Sales role. Using the scorecard approach, they clearly defined the outcomes needed: achieving $10M in sales within the first year, building a team of 10 high-performing salespeople, and establishing partnerships with five major industry players.

Their sourcing efforts involved reaching out to their network and asking specifically for introductions to top-performing sales leaders. Through this process, they identified several potential A-Players who weren't actively job hunting.

In the selection phase, they used the "Who" interview process to dig deep into candidates' past performance and assess their fit with the defined outcomes and competencies. This process revealed that one candidate, while having an impressive resume, lacked experience in building teams - a crucial competency for this role. Another candidate, who might have been overlooked in a traditional process, demonstrated a strong track record in all the key areas.

In the final step, they sold the chosen candidate on the role by emphasizing the opportunity to build something from the ground up and the potential for equity in a high-growth company - factors they had identified as important to the candidate during the interview process.

The result? They successfully hired an A-Player who exceeded the defined outcomes, driving the company to $15M in sales in the first year and building a high-performing team that became a key competitive advantage for the company.

Reflection Questions:

1. *Think about your current hiring process. How does it compare to the "Who" method? What elements could you incorporate to improve your success rate?*

2. *Consider the last person you hired. How would you rate them on the A-Player scale? What could you have done differently in the hiring process to increase your chances of hiring an A-Player?*

3. *What are the potential challenges in implementing the "Who" method in your organization? How might you overcome these challenges?*

As we continue our leadership journey, let's remember that our organizations are only as good as the people within them. By mastering the art of hiring A-Players, we set ourselves and our teams up for exceptional performance and success. In the words of Geoff Smart, "Who you hire is the most important decision you make." Let's commit to making that decision with the care, rigor, and strategy it deserves.

Week 23 - Team Dynamics and Collaboration

"Talent wins games, but teamwork and intelligence wins championships." - Michael Jordan

In our previous chapter, we explored the critical process of hiring A-Players. Now, we turn our attention to how these individuals come together to form high-performing teams. Understanding team dynamics and fostering effective collaboration are essential skills for any leader aiming to maximize their team's potential.

At the heart of team dynamics is Bruce Tuckman's model of group development. This model outlines five stages that teams typically go through:

1. **Forming:** Team members are polite but cautious, trying to orient themselves and figure out their place in the group.
2. **Storming:** Conflicts arise as individuals assert their personalities and vie for position.
3. **Norming:** The team begins to work more effectively as they establish processes and build trust.
4. **Performing:** The team is functioning at a high level, with a focus on reaching goals.
5. **Adjourning:** The team completes its task and prepares to disband.

As leaders, our role is to guide our teams through these stages, providing appropriate support and direction at each phase.

Exercise: Assess Your Team

- Think about your current team.
- Which stage of Tuckman's model best describes where they are?
- What challenges are you facing at this stage?
- What strategies could you employ to help your team progress to the next stage?

Collaboration is the lifeblood of effective teams. However, not everyone collaborates in the same way. Understanding different collaboration styles can help us leverage the diverse strengths of our team members:

1. Contributors focus on getting things done and providing technical expertise.
2. Collaborators emphasize the overall goal and like to pitch in wherever needed.
3. Communicators are process-oriented, focusing on clear communication and inclusion.
4. Challengers ask the tough questions and push the team to take risks and innovate.

A well-functioning team needs a balance of these styles. As leaders, we need to recognize and value these different approaches, ensuring that each style has the opportunity to contribute effectively.

Collaboration Style Self-Assessment:

Reflect on your own collaboration style.

Which of the four styles (Contributor, Collaborator, Communicator, Challenger) do you most identify with?

How does this impact your leadership approach? How can you leverage your style while also appreciating and encouraging other styles in your team?

Take your answers and add them to your PLFM. This information will be very helpful as you work with various teams, clients, and vendors.

Building a collaborative team culture doesn't happen by accident. Here are some strategies to enhance collaboration:

1. **Set clear, shared goals:** Ensure everyone understands and is committed to the team's objectives.
2. **Encourage open communication:** Create an environment where team members feel safe to share ideas and concerns.
3. **Promote mutual accountability:** Foster a culture where team members feel responsible not just for their work, but for the team's overall success.
4. **Celebrate diversity:** Recognize and value the different perspectives and skills each team member brings.

5. **Provide opportunities for bonding:** Both formal team-building activities and informal social interactions can strengthen team cohesion.
6. **Lead by example:** Model the collaborative behaviors you want to see in your team.

Remember, strong team dynamics and effective collaboration don't just make work more enjoyable – they drive better results. Teams that collaborate well are more innovative, more productive, and better able to solve complex problems.

Reflection Questions:

1. *Think about the most collaborative team you've ever been part of. What made that team so effective? How can you bring some of those elements to your current team?*

2. *What's one specific action you can take this week to improve collaboration within your team?*

3. *How might improving team dynamics and collaboration impact your organization's overall performance and culture?*

As we continue our leadership journey, let's remember that our success as leaders is intrinsically tied to the success of our teams. By understanding team dynamics and fostering effective collaboration, we create an environment where both individuals and the collective can thrive. In the words of Henry Ford, "Coming together is a beginning, staying together is progress, and working together is success."

Case Study: The Power of Diverse Collaboration Styles

Consider the case of a product development team at a tech startup. The team was struggling to meet deadlines and produce innovative solutions. Upon analysis, the leader realized that the team was heavily skewed towards Contributors, with everyone heads-down in their individual tasks but little cross-pollination of ideas.

The leader decided to shake things up. She brought in a Challenger from another department to ask tough questions and push the team's thinking. She also identified a natural Communicator within the team and gave them the role of facilitating team meetings and ensuring everyone's voice was heard.

The results were transformative. The Challenger pushed the team to consider new approaches, leading to a breakthrough feature that set their product apart in the market. The Communicator improved information flow, reducing misunderstandings and increasing efficiency. Contributors felt their work was more valued and connected to the bigger picture.

Within three months, the team was not only meeting deadlines but exceeding expectations in terms of innovation and quality.

This case illustrates the power of understanding and leveraging diverse collaboration styles. By ensuring a balance of styles and creating an environment where each style can thrive, we can dramatically improve team performance.

Week 24 - Celebrating Wins and Recognizing Excellence

"People work for money but go the extra mile for recognition, praise and rewards."

- Dale Carnegie

In our previous chapter, we explored the dynamics of effective teams and collaboration. Now, we turn our attention to a critical aspect of leadership that can significantly impact team morale, motivation, and performance: celebrating wins and recognizing excellence.

The power of recognition in the workplace cannot be overstated. Research consistently shows that employees who feel appreciated are more engaged, more productive, and more likely to stay with their organizations. As leaders, our ability to effectively celebrate successes and recognize outstanding contributions can be a game-changer in building high-performing teams.

The Psychology of Recognition

At its core, recognition taps into fundamental human needs: the need to feel valued, to have our efforts acknowledged, and to know that our work matters. When we recognize our team members' achievements, we're not just saying "good job" - we're reinforcing behaviors that contribute to success, boosting confidence, and strengthening the connection between individual efforts and organizational goals.

Recognition can take many forms, from formal awards to informal words of appreciation. It can be public or private, tangible or intangible. The key is that it should be:

1. **Timely:** Recognition should be given as soon as possible after the achievement.
2. **Specific:** Clearly articulate what is being recognized and why it matters.
3. **Sincere:** Authenticity is crucial - insincere praise can do more harm than good.
4. **Proportional:** The recognition should match the level of achievement.
5. **Aligned with individual preferences:** Some people love public praise, while others prefer private acknowledgment.

Case Study: The Power of Meaningful Recognition

Consider the case of a mid-sized marketing agency that was struggling with employee turnover and declining morale. The leadership team decided to overhaul their approach to recognition.

They implemented a multi-faceted strategy:

1. Weekly team meetings now start with each person recognizing a colleague's contribution.
2. A digital "kudos" board was created where employees could publicly appreciate each other.
3. Quarterly awards were established to recognize outstanding performance in various categories.
4. Managers were trained to provide regular, specific feedback and recognition.

The results were remarkable. Within six months, employee satisfaction scores increased by 40%, voluntary turnover decreased by 25%, and client satisfaction improved as more engaged employees delivered higher quality work.

This case illustrates how a thoughtful, consistent approach to recognition can transform an organization's culture and performance.

Developing a Recognition Strategy

As leaders, we need to be intentional about how we celebrate wins and recognize excellence. Here are some key elements to consider in developing your recognition strategy:

1. **Create a culture of appreciation:** Encourage peer-to-peer recognition and make appreciation a regular part of team interactions.
2. **Align recognition with organizational values:** Recognize behaviors and achievements that exemplify your company's core values.
3. **Be specific and timely:** Don't wait for annual reviews to recognize good work. Provide immediate, specific feedback on positive contributions.
4. **Celebrate both individual and team achievements:** While individual recognition is important, don't forget to celebrate team wins.

5. **Use a mix of formal and informal recognition:** From a simple "thank you" to structured award programs, use a variety of methods to recognize excellence.
6. **Make it personal:** Tailor your recognition to the individual's preferences and what would be most meaningful to them.
7. **Follow through:** If you promise recognition or rewards, make sure to deliver on those promises.

Remember, celebrating wins and recognizing excellence isn't just about making people feel good (although that's important too!). It's a powerful tool for reinforcing positive behaviors, building a strong team culture, and driving organizational success.

As you go through your week, look for opportunities to recognize excellence in your team. Pay attention to the impact of your recognition efforts. Notice how timely, specific appreciation can energize individuals and the team as a whole.

Reflection Questions:

1. *Think of the best recognition you've ever received. What made it so impactful? How can you incorporate those elements into your own recognition efforts?*

2. *What's one specific way you could improve how you celebrate wins in your team or organization?*

3. *How might a more robust approach to recognition and celebration impact your team's performance and culture?*

As we continue our leadership journey, let's remember that recognition is not just a nice-to-have - it's a crucial leadership skill that can significantly impact our team's success. In the words of Mary Kay Ash, "There are two things people want more than sex and money: recognition and praise." By mastering the art of celebrating wins and recognizing excellence, we can create more engaged, motivated, and high-performing teams.

Recognition Styles and Celebration Planning:

Take a moment to reflect on your own preferences for recognition. Do you prefer:

- Public praise or private acknowledgment?
- Verbal appreciation or written notes?
- Tangible rewards or new opportunities and responsibilities?

Now think about your team members. Do you know their preferences? If not, how could you find out?

Understanding these preferences can help us tailor our recognition efforts for maximum impact.

Think of a recent win or achievement in your team. How could you celebrate this in a way that:

- Meaningfully recognizes the effort involved
- Reinforces the behaviors that led to the success
- Aligns with your organizational culture and values
- Motivates the team for future challenges

Write down your celebration plan and commit to implementing it in the next week.

Week 25 - After Action Reviews (Army Rangers)

"The only real mistake is the one from which we learn nothing." - Henry Ford

In our previous chapter, we explored the importance of celebrating wins and recognizing excellence. Now, we turn our attention to a powerful tool for continuous improvement that comes from an unexpected source: the U.S. Army Rangers. This tool is the After Action Review (AAR), and it's a structured debrief process that can dramatically enhance learning and performance in any organization.

The concept of AARs was developed by the U.S. Army in the 1970s as a way to learn from both successes and failures in training and combat situations. Since then, it has been adopted by many high-performing organizations outside the military, from hospitals to tech companies, as a way to drive continuous improvement.

At its core, an AAR is a simple but powerful process that asks four key questions:

1. What was expected to happen?
2. What actually happened?
3. Why were there differences?
4. What can we learn from this?

These questions provide a framework for honest, constructive reflection that can yield valuable insights and drive meaningful improvements.

The Principles of Effective AARs

To be truly effective, AARs should adhere to several key principles:

1. **Immediacy:** AARs should be conducted as soon as possible after the event or project, while memories are fresh and lessons are most relevant.
2. **Candor:** Participants must feel safe to speak honestly about what happened, without fear of blame or retribution.
3. **Learning Focus:** The goal is not to assign blame, but to identify lessons that can improve future performance.
4. **Inclusivity**: AARs should involve all key participants, regardless of rank or role.
5. **Action-Oriented:** The insights gained should lead to concrete actions or changes.

Case Study: AARs in Action

Consider the case of a software development team that was consistently missing project deadlines. The team leader decided to implement AARs after each sprint.

In their first AAR, the team discovered several issues:

- Expectations weren't clearly communicated at the start of the sprint
- Unexpected technical challenges arose that weren't quickly escalated
- Team members were hesitant to ask for help when stuck

Based on these insights, the team implemented several changes:

- They created a more detailed sprint kickoff process
- They established a daily stand-up meeting to catch issues early
- They paired junior and senior developers to encourage knowledge sharing

The results were significant. Over the next three months, the team met all their sprint goals and improved their velocity by 30%. More importantly, team morale improved as members felt more supported and better able to contribute to the team's success.

This case illustrates how AARs can drive tangible improvements in performance and team dynamics.

Implementing AARs in Your Organization

While the concept of AARs is simple, implementing them effectively can be challenging. Here are some strategies to consider:

1. **Start Small:** Begin with AARs for specific projects or events before rolling them out more broadly.
2. **Create Psychological Safety:** Foster an environment where team members feel safe to speak honestly about what happened.
3. **Focus on Systems, Not Individuals:** Look for systemic issues rather than individual mistakes.
4. **Document and Share Learnings:** Ensure insights from AARs are captured and shared with relevant stakeholders.
5. **Follow Through:** Create action plans based on AAR insights and track their implementation.

6. **Lead by Example:** As a leader, participate openly in AARs and model the behavior you want to see.

Overcoming Common AAR Challenges

Implementing AARs can face several challenges:

1. **Time Constraints**: In busy environments, it can be tempting to skip AARs. Combat this by scheduling them in advance and keeping them concise.
2. **Defensiveness:** Some team members may feel threatened by the AAR process. Address this by emphasizing the learning focus and modeling openness to feedback.
3. **Lack of Follow-Through:** Ensure AAR insights lead to concrete actions by assigning responsibility for follow-up and regularly reviewing progress.

As you go through your week, look for opportunities to implement AARs in your team or organization. Pay attention to how this structured reflection process can uncover valuable insights and drive meaningful improvements.

Reflection Questions:

1. *Think of a recent project or initiative in your organization. How might an AAR have improved the outcome or learning from that experience?*

2. *What potential challenges do you foresee in implementing AARs in your team or organization? How might you overcome these challenges?*

3. *How could regular use of AARs impact your team's performance and culture of continuous improvement?*

As we continue our leadership journey, let's remember that true learning often comes from structured reflection on our experiences, both successes and failures. By adopting the AAR process, we can create a culture of continuous improvement, where every experience becomes an opportunity for growth and enhancement. In the words of John Dewey, *"We do not learn from experience... we learn from reflecting on experience."*

Exercise: Conducting a Personal AAR

Think about a recent project or significant event in your work. Take a few minutes to conduct a personal AAR:

1. What was expected to happen?
2. What actually happened?
3. Why were there differences?
4. What can you learn from this?

Write down your insights and at least one action you can take based on what you've learned.

Part 3:

Strategy and Execution

Week 26 - Crafting a Compelling Vision (John Kotter)

"Vision is the art of seeing what is invisible to others." - Jonathan Swift

In our previous chapter, we explored the importance of After Action Reviews in learning from experiences and improving team performance. Now, we turn our attention to a critical aspect of leadership that sets the direction for all our efforts: crafting a compelling vision. As leaders, our ability to create and communicate a clear, inspiring vision can make the difference between a team that merely performs tasks and one that is driven by a sense of purpose and direction.

A compelling vision is not just a nice-to-have; it's a fundamental element of effective leadership. It provides a clear picture of what success looks like, aligns efforts across the organization, and inspires people to give their best. As John Kotter, a renowned leadership expert, emphasizes, vision is a crucial component of leading change and driving organizational success.

Let's start by exploring some key principles of crafting a compelling vision:

1. **Clarity and Simplicity:** A vision should be clear and easy to understand. It should be concise enough to be easily remembered and repeated.
2. **Inspirational and Aspirational:** A vision should stretch beyond the current reality, inspiring people to reach for something greater.
3. **Aligned with Core Values:** The vision should reflect and reinforce the organization's fundamental beliefs and principles.
4. **Focused on the Future:** While rooted in the present, a vision should paint a picture of a desirable future state.
5. **Stakeholder-Oriented:** Consider how the vision impacts and appeals to all stakeholders - employees, customers, shareholders, and the community.

Exercise 1: Vision Statement Workshop

In small groups, craft a vision statement for your organization or department. Use the following prompts:

1. What is the ultimate purpose of your organization?

2. What impact do you want to have on your customers, employees, and community?
3. What will success look like in 5-10 years?

After crafting your vision statements, share them with the larger group and discuss:

- How well do they embody the principles of a compelling vision?
- What was challenging about the process?
- How might these visions inspire and guide your teams?

Now, let's turn our attention to communicating and implementing the vision. As Kotter points out in his 8-step process for leading change, creating a vision is just the beginning. The real challenge lies in effectively communicating it and aligning the organization around it.

Here are some key strategies for vision communication and implementation:

1. **Repetition:** Share the vision frequently and consistently across various channels.
2. **Lead by Example:** Demonstrate commitment to the vision through your actions and decisions.
3. **Connect to Daily Work:** Help team members understand how their roles contribute to the larger vision.
4. **Encourage Feedback:** Create opportunities for dialogue about the vision and be open to input.
5. **Celebrate Progress:** Recognize and reward efforts that align with and advance the vision.

Exercise 2: Vision Communication Plan

Develop a plan to communicate your vision effectively:

1. Identify key stakeholders
2. Choose appropriate communication channels for each stakeholder group
3. Create a timeline for rolling out the vision
4. Design methods to gather feedback and measure understanding

Share your plans with a partner and discuss potential challenges and strategies to overcome them.

Developing Your Vision-Crafting Skills

Improving your ability to craft and communicate compelling visions is an ongoing process. Here are some strategies to help you continue developing:

- **Study Visionary Leaders:** Read about or watch speeches from leaders known for their compelling visions.
- **Practice Storytelling:** A vision often becomes more powerful when wrapped in a narrative.
- **Seek Diverse Input:** Engage with people at all levels of your organization to inform your vision.
- **Refine and Adapt:** Regularly revisit and refine your vision as circumstances change.
- **Measure Impact:** Look for ways to assess how well your vision is understood and inspiring action.

As you go through your week, pay attention to how vision is communicated in your workplace. Is there a clear, compelling vision? How is it reinforced? Look for opportunities to discuss and reinforce the vision with your team.

Remember, as Antoine de Saint-Exupéry said, *"If you want to build a ship, don't drum up people to collect wood and don't assign them tasks and work, but rather teach them to long for the endless immensity of the sea."* In the same way, our role as leaders is not just to assign tasks, but to create a vision that inspires our teams to see beyond the immediate and strive for something greater.

Reflection Questions:

1. *Think of a leader you admire. What makes their vision compelling? How do they communicate it effectively?*

2. *How well does your current organizational vision align with the principles we've discussed? What could be improved?*

3. *In what ways could a more compelling vision impact your team's motivation and performance?*

As we continue our leadership journey, let's embrace the power of vision to inspire, align, and drive our organizations forward. By mastering the art of crafting and communicating compelling visions, we can create more purposeful, motivated, and high-performing teams.

Week 27 - Goal Setting and Achieving BHAGs (Jim Collins)

"If you can dream it, you can do it." - Walt Disney

In our previous chapter, we explored the art of crafting a compelling vision. Now, we turn our attention to a crucial aspect of bringing that vision to life: setting and achieving Big Hairy Audacious Goals (BHAGs). Coined by Jim Collins and Jerry Porras in their book *Built to Last*, BHAGs are ambitious, long-term goals that have the power to transform organizations and inspire extraordinary effort.

As leaders, our ability to set and pursue BHAGs can be the difference between incremental progress and transformative success. BHAGs push us beyond our comfort zones, align our efforts, and create a sense of excitement and purpose that can energize entire organizations.

Let's start by exploring the key characteristics of effective BHAGs:

1. **BIG:** They should stretch beyond current capabilities and comfort zones.
2. **HAIRY:** They should be challenging and perhaps a bit daunting.
3. **AUDACIOUS:** They should be bold and exciting.
4. **GOAL:** They should have a clear finish line and time frame.

BHAGs are not just oversized quarterly objectives. They are long-term (10-30 year) goals that require sustained effort and often fundamental changes in how an organization operates.

BHAG Brainstorming Session:

In small groups, brainstorm potential BHAGs for your organization or department. Consider:

1. What would be truly game-changing for your industry?
2. What audacious goal would energize and unite your team?
3. How can you push beyond incremental improvements?

After brainstorming, share your ideas with the larger group and discuss:

- How well do these potential BHAGs embody the BHAG characteristics?

- Which ones seem most inspiring and why?

- What challenges might you face in pursuing these BHAGs?

Now, let's turn our attention to the process of setting and pursuing BHAGs. It's not enough to simply declare an audacious goal; we need a strategy to achieve it.

Here are some key strategies for setting and achieving BHAGs:

1. **Align with Core Values and Purpose:** BHAGs should be consistent with your organization's fundamental beliefs and reason for existence.

2. **Break It Down:** While the BHAG is long-term, break it down into medium-term goals and short-term objectives.

3. **Create a Vivid Description:** Paint a clear picture of what achieving the BHAG will look like.

4. **Communicate Relentlessly:** Share the BHAG frequently and connect it to daily activities.

5. **Track Progress:** Develop metrics to measure progress towards the BHAG.

6. **Celebrate Milestones:** Recognize and reward efforts that move you closer to the BHAG.

BHAG Implementation Plan:

Choose one BHAG from your brainstorming session and create a high-level implementation plan:

1. Break down the BHAG into smaller, medium-term goals
2. Identify key milestones and metrics

3. Outline potential challenges and strategies to overcome them
4. Determine resources needed and potential partnerships

Share your plans with a partner and discuss how you might refine and improve them.

Developing Your BHAG-Setting Skills

Improving your ability to set and pursue BHAGs is an ongoing process. Here are some strategies to help you continue developing:

- **Study BHAG Success Stories:** Research organizations that have achieved remarkable BHAGs and learn from their experiences.
- **Practice Long-Term Thinking:** Regularly engage in exercises that push you to think 10, 20, or 30 years into the future.
- **Cultivate a Growth Mindset:** Embrace challenges and view failures as learning opportunities.
- **Build a Culture of Ambition:** Encourage your team to think big and propose audacious ideas.
- **Stay Committed but Flexible:** Be willing to adjust your approach as circumstances change, but stay committed to the ultimate goal.

As you go through your week, pay attention to the goals being set in your workplace. Are they truly stretching the organization? How might introducing a BHAG change the energy and focus of your team?

Remember, as Jim Collins said, *"Good is the enemy of great."* BHAGs push us beyond good and towards greatness. They challenge us to dream bigger, work harder, and achieve more than we ever thought possible.

Reflection Questions:

1. *Think of a time when you or your organization achieved something you initially thought was impossible. What made it possible?*

2. *How might pursuing a BHAG change the culture and performance of your team or organization?*

3. *What personal BHAG could you set for yourself that aligns with your organization's goals?*

As we continue our leadership journey, let's embrace the power of BHAGs to inspire, challenge, and transform our organizations. By mastering the art of setting and pursuing audacious goals, we can unlock new levels of performance and achievement, turning the seemingly impossible into reality.

Video Break: Jim Collins Answers some good questions:

- Question #3: How can you reframe failure as growth, in pursuit of a BHAG? (3 min)
  [https://youtu.be/6OJS7V9MnS8?feature=shared]

- Question #5: Have you found your hedgehog -- your personal hedgehog? (2 min)
  [https://youtu.be/ERcF9HKmjh0?feature=shared]

Reflection Questions:

1. *What is your Hedgehog?*

2. *How are you going to look at failure going forward from today?*

Week 28 - Strategic Planning Best Practices

"In preparing for battle I have always found that plans are useless, but planning is indispensable." - Dwight D. Eisenhower

In our previous chapter, we explored the power of setting Big Hairy Audacious Goals (BHAGs). Now, we turn our attention to the critical process of strategic planning - the bridge that connects our ambitious visions and goals to actionable plans and measurable results.

Strategic planning is not just an annual ritual; it's a dynamic, ongoing process that helps organizations define their direction and make decisions on allocating resources to pursue this direction. As leaders, our ability to guide effective strategic planning can make the difference between an organization that merely reacts to its environment and one that proactively shapes its future.

Let's start by exploring the key components of an effective strategic plan:

1. **Mission and Vision Statements:** The foundation that defines why your organization exists and what it aspires to become.
2. **SWOT Analysis:** An assessment of Strengths, Weaknesses, Opportunities, and Threats.
3. **Long-term Goals and Objectives:** Specific, measurable targets aligned with your mission and vision.
4. **Action Plans:** Detailed steps to achieve your objectives.
5. **Resource Allocation:** How you'll deploy people, finances, and other resources.
6. **Key Performance Indicators (KPIs):** Metrics to track progress and success.

Exercise: SWOT Analysis Workshop

In small groups, conduct a SWOT analysis for your organization or department:

1. Strengths: Internal factors that give you an advantage
2. Weaknesses: Internal factors that put you at a disadvantage
3. Opportunities: External factors you could exploit to your advantage
4. Threats: External factors that could cause trouble for your business

After completing the analysis, share with the larger group and discuss:

- What surprising insights emerged from this exercise?
- How might this SWOT analysis inform your strategic planning?
- What potential strategies could leverage strengths and opportunities while addressing weaknesses and threats?

Now, let's turn our attention to best practices in the strategic planning process:

1. **Involve Key Stakeholders:** Engage people at various levels of the organization to gain diverse perspectives and build buy-in.
2. **Use Data-Driven Decision Making:** Base your strategies on solid research and analysis, not just intuition.
3. **Align with Organizational Culture:** Ensure your strategies are compatible with your company's values and ways of working.
4. **Develop Contingency Plans:** Prepare for potential obstacles and changes in the environment.
5. **Communicate the Plan Effectively:** Ensure everyone understands their role in executing the strategy.
6. **Review and Adjust Regularly:** Treat the strategic plan as a living document, revisiting and updating it as needed.

Try This: Strategic Initiative Prioritization

List potential strategic initiatives for your organization and prioritize them using the following criteria:

1. Alignment with organizational goals
2. Potential impact
3. Resource requirements
4. Feasibility and risk
5. Time to implement

Create a prioritized list of initiatives and discuss the rationale behind your choices with a partner.

Developing Your Strategic Planning Skills

Improving your strategic planning abilities is an ongoing process. Here are some strategies to help you continue developing:

- **Study Successful Strategies:** Analyze case studies of organizations known for effective strategic planning.
- **Practice Scenario Planning:** Regularly engage in exercises that consider multiple possible futures.
- **Enhance Your Financial Acumen:** Improve your understanding of financial metrics and their strategic implications.
- **Cultivate Systems Thinking:** Practice seeing the interconnections between different parts of your organization and industry.
- **Stay Informed:** Keep up with trends and changes in your industry and the broader business environment.

As you go through your week, pay attention to how strategic decisions are made in your organization. Are they aligned with a clear plan? How might improving the strategic planning process enhance decision-making and results?

Remember, as Michael Porter said, "The essence of strategy is choosing what not to do." Effective strategic planning isn't just about deciding what to do, but also what to prioritize and what to let go.

Reflection Questions:

1. *Think of a time when a lack of strategic planning led to challenges in your organization. What could have been done differently?*

2. *How well does your current strategic planning process incorporate the best practices we've discussed? What could be improved?*

3. *In what ways could more effective strategic planning impact your team's focus and performance?*

As we continue our leadership journey, let's embrace the power of strategic planning to guide our organizations towards success. By mastering the art of translating vision into actionable plans, we can create more focused, adaptable, and high-performing organizations ready to thrive in an ever-changing business landscape.

Case Study: Revitalizing Midwest Manufacturing

Midwest Manufacturing, a mid-sized company producing industrial equipment, had been experiencing stagnant growth and declining market share for several years. The CEO, Sarah Thompson, recognized the need for a comprehensive strategic planning process to turn the company around.

Sarah assembled a diverse team from various departments and levels within the organization to participate in the strategic planning process. They began with a thorough SWOT analysis, which revealed:

Strengths:

- Strong engineering capabilities
- Loyal customer base in traditional markets
- Efficient production processes

Weaknesses:

- Outdated product line
- Limited presence in emerging markets

- Aging workforce with potential skills gap

Opportunities:

- Growing demand for eco-friendly industrial equipment
- Potential for expansion into Asian markets
- Emerging technologies in IoT and AI for manufacturing

Threats:

- Increasing competition from low-cost overseas manufacturers
- Rapidly changing technology in the industry
- Economic uncertainty in key markets

Based on this analysis, the team developed a five-year strategic plan with the following key components:

1. Product Innovation: Invest in R&D to develop a new line of eco-friendly, smart-enabled equipment.
2. Market Expansion: Establish a presence in Asian markets, starting with a sales office and moving towards local manufacturing.
3. Workforce Development: Implement a comprehensive training program and recruit young talent to address the skills gap.
4. Digital Transformation: Integrate IoT and AI technologies into both products and manufacturing processes.
5. Sustainability Initiative: Position the company as a leader in sustainable manufacturing practices.

The team set specific, measurable goals for each of these initiatives and developed detailed action plans. They also established KPIs to track progress, including market share, revenue growth, employee skills assessments, and sustainability metrics.

Sarah ensured that the plan was communicated clearly throughout the organization and that each department understood its role in executing the strategy. She also committed to quarterly review meetings to assess progress and make necessary adjustments.

Two years into the implementation of this strategic plan, Midwest Manufacturing has seen a 15% increase in revenue, expanded into two new Asian markets, and launched a successful line of eco-friendly smart equipment. Employee engagement scores have also improved significantly.

Reflection Questions:

1. How did the SWOT analysis inform Midwest Manufacturing's strategic planning process? Can you identify specific strategies that address elements of the SWOT?

2. In what ways did Midwest Manufacturing's strategic planning process align with the best practices discussed in this week's lesson?

3. How might the involvement of a diverse team in the strategic planning process have contributed to its success? What potential challenges might this approach present?

4. Consider the KPIs mentioned in the case study. Are there any additional metrics you would suggest to track the success of this strategic plan?

5. The case mentions quarterly review meetings. How important do you think this regular review and adjustment process is to the success of a strategic plan? How would you structure these reviews in your organization?

6. Reflecting on your own organization, are there elements of Midwest Manufacturing's approach that you could apply to improve your strategic planning process?

Week 29 - Agile Project Management (Jeff Sutherland)

"The art of maximizing the amount of work not done is essential." - Agile Manifesto

In our previous chapter, we explored strategic planning best practices. Now, we turn our attention to a methodology that has revolutionized project management and product development: Agile. Specifically, we'll focus on Scrum, an Agile framework developed by Jeff Sutherland and Ken Schwaber.

As leaders in today's fast-paced business environment, our ability to adapt quickly to change and deliver value incrementally can make the difference between success and failure. Agile methodologies, particularly Scrum, provide a framework for doing just that.

Let's start by exploring the key principles of Agile:

1. Individuals and interactions over processes and tools
2. Working software over comprehensive documentation
3. Customer collaboration over contract negotiation
4. Responding to change over following a plan

These principles emphasize flexibility, collaboration, and customer focus - all crucial elements in today's business landscape.

Now, let's dive into the Scrum framework, which includes three key roles:

1. Product Owner: Represents the stakeholders and is the voice of the customer
2. Scrum Master: Ensures the team follows Agile principles and practices
3. Development Team: Cross-functional group that delivers the product

Scrum Role Play:

Form groups of 5-7 people and assign the Scrum roles. Create a hypothetical project and conduct a 15-minute sprint planning session. After the exercise, discuss:

- How did it feel to work in these defined roles?
- What challenges did you encounter?
- How might this structure benefit your current projects?

Scrum is built around the concept of "sprints" - short, time-boxed periods where a specific set of work is completed and made ready for review. The Scrum events include:

1. **Sprint Planning**: Team decides what can be delivered in the sprint and how
2. **Daily Scrum:** 15-minute daily meeting to synchronize activities
3. **Sprint Review:** Team presents work to stakeholders for feedback
4. **Sprint Retrospective:** Team reflects on the past sprint and identifies improvements

The benefits of Agile project management include:

- Increased flexibility and adaptability
- Faster time-to-market
- Higher customer satisfaction
- Improved team morale and productivity
- Better risk management

Agile Transformation Plan:

Develop a high-level plan to implement Agile practices in your organization or department:

1. Identify areas where Agile could be beneficial
2. Outline necessary cultural and structural changes
3. Determine training and resource needs
4. Create a timeline for gradual implementation
5. Establish metrics to measure the impact of Agile adoption

Share your plans with a partner and discuss potential challenges and strategies to overcome them.

Developing Your Agile Leadership Skills

Improving your ability to lead in an Agile environment is an ongoing process. Here are some strategies to help you continue developing:

- **Embrace Servant Leadership:** Focus on removing obstacles for your team

- **Foster Transparency:** Encourage open communication and visibility of work
- **Promote Self-Organization:** Trust your team to make decisions
- **Emphasize Continuous Improvement:** Always look for ways to enhance processes and outcomes
- **Stay Flexible:** Be willing to adapt plans based on new information

As you go through your week, pay attention to how projects are managed in your organization. Are there opportunities to introduce Agile methodologies? How might this change the way work is done and results are achieved?

Remember, as Jeff Sutherland said, "The minimum plan necessary to start a Scrum project consists of a vision and a Product Backlog. The vision describes why the project is being undertaken and what the desired end state is."

Reflection Questions:

1. *How might adopting Agile methodologies change the culture of your organization?*

2. *What potential challenges do you foresee in implementing Agile practices in your current environment?*

3. *How could Agile principles be applied beyond software development in your organization?*

As we continue our leadership journey, let's embrace the power of Agile methodologies to create more responsive, customer-focused, and efficient organizations. By mastering Agile project management, we can lead our teams to deliver value more quickly and adapt more readily to our ever-changing business landscape.

Week 30 - Metrics, KPIs and Dashboards

"What gets measured gets managed." - Peter Drucker

In our previous chapter, we explored Agile project management methodologies. Now, we turn our attention to a critical aspect of leadership and management: measuring performance through metrics, Key Performance Indicators (KPIs), and dashboards. As leaders, our ability to select, track, and interpret the right metrics can make the difference between informed decision-making and flying blind.

Let's start by exploring the key principles of effective measurement:

1. **Alignment with Strategy:** Metrics should directly tie to your organization's goals and objectives.
2. **Actionability:** Focus on metrics that you can influence through your actions.
3. **Balance:** Use a mix of leading (predictive) and lagging (outcome) indicators.
4. **Simplicity:** Keep your metrics clear and easy to understand.
5. **Timeliness:** Ensure data is available when you need it to make decisions.

Now, let's dive into the different types of metrics:

1. **Financial Metrics:** Revenue, profit margins, return on investment
2. **Customer Metrics:** Satisfaction scores, retention rates, Net Promoter Score
3. **Internal Process Metrics:** Cycle time, defect rates, productivity
4. **Learning and Growth Metrics:** Employee engagement, innovation rates, skills development

Try This: KPI Development Workshop

This workshop will help you develop the crucial skill of creating effective KPIs:

1. Divide into small groups of 3-4 people.
2. Choose a fictional or real business scenario.
3. Identify 3-5 key strategic objectives for this business.
4. For each objective, brainstorm potential metrics.
5. Evaluate each metric based on relevance, measurability, and actionability.
6. Select the most appropriate KPI for each objective.

7. Define targets and measurement frequency for each KPI.
8. Present your KPIs to the larger group and discuss your rationale.

This exercise will enhance your ability to align metrics with strategic goals and select meaningful KPIs.

Video Break: Why the Secret to Success is Setting the Right Goals | John Doerr (12 min)
[https://youtu.be/L4N1q4RNi9I]

This video provides practical insights on creating effective KPIs or OKRs and avoiding common pitfalls.

1. What are some potential challenges in implementing OKRs that Doerr addresses in his talk?
2. How does the OKR system relate to our discussion of KPIs and metrics in this chapter?
3. Based on Doerr's presentation, how might you adapt or improve your current goal-setting and measurement practices?

Case Study: Revitalizing Retail with Data-Driven Decisions

RetailCo, a mid-sized clothing retailer, was struggling with declining sales and customer loyalty. The new CEO, Sarah Chen, implemented a data-driven approach to turn the company around.

Sarah introduced a balanced scorecard with carefully selected KPIs:

1. Financial: Sales per square foot, gross margin
2. Customer: Net Promoter Score, repeat purchase rate

3. Internal Process: Inventory turnover, average transaction time
4. Learning and Growth: Employee satisfaction, training hours per employee

She also implemented a user-friendly dashboard that provided real-time updates on these metrics to all store managers.

Within six months, RetailCo saw significant improvements:

- Sales per square foot increased by 15%
- Net Promoter Score rose from 30 to 45
- Inventory turnover improved by 20%
- Employee satisfaction scores increased by 25%

The data-driven approach allowed store managers to make informed decisions quickly. For example, noticing a low inventory turnover for certain items prompted timely markdowns, improving cash flow and making space for better-selling products.

This case demonstrates how well-chosen metrics and effective dashboards can drive performance improvements across multiple areas of a business.

Reflection Questions:

1. *How well do your current organizational metrics align with your strategic objectives?*

2. *What behaviors might your current metrics be inadvertently encouraging or discouraging?*

3. *How could better use of metrics and dashboards improve decision-making in your organization?*

As we continue our leadership journey, let's embrace the power of metrics, KPIs, and dashboards to drive performance and inform decision-making. By mastering these tools, we can create more data-driven, transparent, and high-performing organizations ready to thrive in our increasingly complex business environment.

Week 31 - Problem Solving Methodologies (McKinsey)

"The formulation of a problem is often more essential than its solution." - Albert Einstein

In our journey through leadership development, we've explored various crucial skills and concepts. This week, we turn our attention to a fundamental capability that underpins effective leadership: structured problem-solving. Specifically, we'll delve into the problem-solving methodologies used by top consulting firms like McKinsey & Company, which have been refined and proven effective across industries and challenges.

The Importance of Structured Problem-Solving

As leaders, we face complex challenges daily. The ability to approach these challenges systematically, break them down into manageable components, and develop effective solutions is invaluable. Structured problem-solving methodologies provide a framework that can be applied to a wide range of issues, from strategic decisions to operational improvements.

The McKinsey Problem-Solving Process

McKinsey's approach to problem-solving is renowned for its rigor and effectiveness. Let's explore the key steps in this process:

1. **Define the Problem**: This crucial first step involves clearly articulating the issue at hand. A well-defined problem statement sets the direction for the entire problem-solving process. It should be specific, measurable, and focused on the core issue.
2. **Structure the Problem:** Once the problem is defined, it needs to be broken down into its component parts. This step involves identifying the key drivers and factors influencing the problem.
3. **Prioritize Issues:** Not all aspects of a problem are equally important. This step involves determining which issues are most critical to address.
4. **Analyze the Issues:** This step involves gathering and analyzing data related to the prioritized issues. It's about understanding the root causes and relationships between different factors.
5. **Synthesize Findings:** After analysis, the next step is to bring together the insights gained to form a coherent picture of the situation.
6. **Develop Recommendations:** Based on the synthesis of findings, develop clear, actionable recommendations to address the problem.
7. **Communicate and Implement Solutions:** The final step involves effectively communicating the recommendations and implementing the chosen solutions.

Key Problem-Solving Tools

To support this process, McKinsey and other top consulting firms use a variety of tools. Let's explore some of the most important ones:

1. **MECE (Mutually Exclusive, Collectively Exhaustive) Principle:** This principle ensures that problem components are broken down without overlap (mutually exclusive) while covering all possibilities (collectively exhaustive). It's crucial for structuring problems effectively.
2. **Issue Trees and Logic Trees:** These visual tools help break down problems into increasingly specific components. They're particularly useful in the problem structuring phase.
3. **Hypothesis-Driven Thinking:** This approach involves forming initial hypotheses about the problem and its solutions, then testing these hypotheses through data collection and analysis. It helps focus the problem-solving effort and ensures a rigorous, evidence-based approach.
4. **80/20 Rule (Pareto Principle):** This principle suggests that roughly 80% of effects come from 20% of causes. In problem-solving, it helps focus efforts on the most impactful areas.
5. **Root Cause Analysis (5 Whys):** This technique involves repeatedly asking "why" to dig deeper into the root causes of a problem. It's particularly useful in understanding complex, multi-layered issues.
6. **External System Analysis:** This involves examining how external factors and systems impact the problem at hand. It ensures a comprehensive view of the problem context.

Applying These Methodologies in Leadership

As leaders, incorporating these problem-solving methodologies into our approach can significantly enhance our effectiveness. Here are some ways to apply these concepts:

1. **Foster a Problem-Solving Culture:** Encourage your team to approach challenges systematically. Introduce these methodologies and tools in team meetings and problem-solving sessions.
2. **Ask the Right Questions:** Use the MECE principle and issue trees to ensure you're considering all aspects of a problem. Train yourself to ask probing questions that uncover root causes.
3. **Data-Driven Decision Making:** Emphasize the importance of data in testing hypotheses and making decisions. Create processes that facilitate data collection and analysis.
4. **Prioritization:** Use the 80/20 rule to focus team efforts on the most impactful areas. This can improve efficiency and effectiveness across your organization.
5. **Continuous Improvement:** Regularly revisit past decisions and solutions. Use the 5 Whys technique to understand any shortcomings and drive continuous improvement.

6. **Holistic Thinking:** Incorporate external system analysis to ensure you're considering the broader context of your challenges and decisions.

By mastering these problem-solving methodologies, you'll be better equipped to tackle the complex challenges that come with leadership. You'll be able to approach problems more systematically, make more informed decisions, and ultimately drive better outcomes for your team and organization.

Remember, like any skill, effective problem-solving improves with practice. Consciously apply these methods to your daily challenges, and over time, you'll find yourself naturally approaching problems in a more structured, effective manner.

Try This: Problem Structuring Workshop

Objective: To practice breaking down complex problems using the MECE principle and issue trees.

Instructions:

1. Choose a current challenge facing your organization or department.
2. Spend 10 minutes individually creating an issue tree for this problem. Remember to apply the MECE principle.
3. In small groups of 3-4, share your issue trees and discuss the different approaches.
4. As a group, create a consolidated issue tree that incorporates the best elements from each individual's work.
5. Identify the top 3-5 issues that you believe would have the greatest impact if addressed (applying the 80/20 rule).
6. Present your final issue tree and prioritized issues to the larger group.

Reflection:

- How did using an issue tree change your understanding of the problem?
- In what ways did the MECE principle help in structuring the problem?
- How might this approach be useful in your day-to-day leadership responsibilities?

Reflection Questions:

1. *How does your current approach to problem-solving compare to the structured methodologies we've discussed? What elements might you incorporate to enhance your approach?*

2. *Think of a recent complex challenge you faced as a leader. How might applying the McKinsey problem-solving process have changed your approach or the outcome?*

3. *Which of the problem-solving tools (MECE, issue trees, hypothesis-driven thinking, 80/20 rule, 5 Whys, or external system analysis) do you find most intriguing or potentially useful? Why?*

Try This: Root Cause Analysis Self-Reflection

Objective: To apply the 5 Whys technique to a personal or professional challenge.

Instructions:

1. Identify a recurring problem or challenge you face in your leadership role.
2. Write down the problem statement clearly and concisely.
3. Ask yourself "Why is this happening?" and write down the answer.
4. For each answer, ask "Why?" again. Repeat this process at least five times.
5. Review your chain of whys. Have you reached a root cause, or do you need to dig deeper?
6. Based on the root cause(s) you've identified, brainstorm potential solutions.
7. Share your analysis with a partner or small group, discussing insights and potential actions.

Reflection:

- How did this process change your understanding of the problem?
- Were you surprised by any of the root causes you uncovered?
- How might regularly applying this technique impact your leadership effectiveness?

Week 32 - Decision Making Frameworks

"The best way to predict your future is to create it." - Peter Drucker

Last week, we explored problem-solving methodologies. This week, we'll build on that foundation by examining decision-making frameworks. As leaders, the quality of our decisions often determines the success of our teams and organizations. Understanding and applying robust decision-making frameworks can significantly enhance our leadership effectiveness.

The Importance of Structured Decision Making

In today's complex and fast-paced business environment, leaders are constantly called upon to make decisions, often with incomplete information and under time pressure. Structured decision-making frameworks provide a systematic approach to evaluating options, considering consequences, and ultimately making choices that align with organizational goals and values.

Key Decision-Making Frameworks

1. **Rational Decision-Making Model:**
   This classic model follows a logical, step-by-step process:
   a. Identify the decision to be made
   b. Gather relevant information
   c. Identify alternatives
   d. Weigh the evidence
   e. Choose among alternatives
   f. Take action
   g. Review decision and consequences

   While thorough, this model assumes perfect information and rationality, which isn't always realistic in complex business situations.

2. **Bounded Rationality Model:**
   Developed by Herbert Simon, this model recognizes that decision-makers have limitations (bounds) on their ability to gather and process information. It suggests that we often make satisficing (satisfactory and sufficing) decisions rather than optimal ones.

3. **Vroom-Yetton-Jago Decision Model:**
   This model focuses on the degree of participation in decision-making. It helps leaders choose the appropriate level of involvement from team members based on the nature of the decision and the context.

4. **Recognition-Primed Decision (RPD) Model:**
Developed for high-pressure situations, this model suggests that experienced decision-makers often make rapid decisions based on recognizing similar situations from their past experience.

5. **Ethical Decision-Making Framework:**
This framework incorporates ethical considerations into the decision-making process:
    a. Identify the ethical issues
    b. Get the facts
    c. Evaluate alternative actions from various ethical perspectives
    d. Make a decision and test it
    e. Act and reflect on the outcome

6. **OODA Loop (Observe, Orient, Decide, Act):**
Developed by military strategist John Boyd, this model is particularly useful in fast-changing environments. It emphasizes the importance of quick adaptation and decision-making in response to changing circumstances.

Try This: Ethical Decision-Making Scenario

1. Read the following scenario: Your company has developed a new product that could significantly increase profits. However, you've discovered that while it meets all current regulations, it may have long-term environmental impacts that are not yet regulated. Releasing the product now would give you a significant market advantage.
2. Apply the Ethical Decision-Making Framework:
    a. Identify the ethical issues
    b. Get the facts
    c. Evaluate alternative actions from various ethical perspectives
    d. Make a decision and test it
    e. Act and reflect on the outcome
3. Share your analysis and decision with a partner or small group. Discuss the challenges and considerations in making this decision.

Tools to Support Decision Making

1. **Decision Matrix:** A tool that allows comparison of multiple options based on weighted criteria.
2. **Cost-Benefit Analysis:** A systematic approach for calculating and comparing the costs and benefits of different options.
3. **SWOT Analysis:** A strategic planning tool that identifies Strengths, Weaknesses, Opportunities, and Threats related to business competition or project planning.
4. **Scenario Planning:** A method for visualizing different future scenarios to prepare for various possible outcomes.
5. **Delphi Technique:** A method of gathering expert opinions through a series of questionnaires and feedback.

Applying Decision-Making Frameworks in Leadership

1. **Choose the Right Framework:** Different situations call for different approaches. High-stakes, complex decisions might benefit from the Rational Model, while rapid, high-pressure decisions might be better served by the RPD Model.
2. **Involve the Right People:** Use the Vroom-Yetton-Jago model to determine when and how to involve team members in decisions.
3. **Consider Ethical Implications:** Incorporate the Ethical Decision-Making Framework, especially for decisions with significant stakeholder impact.
4. **Embrace Uncertainty:** Use tools like Scenario Planning to prepare for various possible outcomes.
5. **Balance Analysis and Intuition:** While data-driven decision making is crucial, don't discount the value of experience and intuition, especially in complex or ambiguous situations.
6. **Learn from Decisions:** Regularly review the outcomes of your decisions to refine your decision-making process.

Try This: Decision Matrix Workshop

Objective: To practice using a decision matrix for a complex decision.

Instructions:

1. Identify a significant decision you're currently facing in your leadership role.

2. List 3-5 possible options or solutions.
3. Determine 4-6 key criteria for evaluating these options (e.g., cost, time to implement, potential impact, risk).
4. Create a decision matrix: list options as rows and criteria as columns.
5. Assign a weight to each criterion (1-10, with 10 being most important).
6. Score each option against each criterion (1-10, with 10 being best).
7. Multiply each score by the criterion weight and sum the results for each option.
8. Discuss the results. Does the highest-scoring option align with your intuition? Why or why not?

Reflection Questions:

1. *Which decision-making framework do you find yourself using most often? How might incorporating other frameworks enhance your decision-making process?*

2. *Think of a recent important decision you made. How might the outcome have been different if you had applied one of the frameworks discussed in this chapter?*

3. *How can you balance the need for thorough analysis in decision-making with the often-pressing need for quick decisions in today's fast-paced business environment?*

By mastering these decision-making frameworks and tools, you'll be better equipped to navigate the complex challenges of leadership, making more informed, ethical, and effective decisions that drive your organization forward.

Week 33 - Risk Management and Contingency Planning

"In preparing for battle I have always found that plans are useless, but planning is indispensable." - Dwight D. Eisenhower

As we near the end of our leadership journey, it's crucial to address a skill that can make or break your success as a leader: risk management and contingency planning. In an ever-changing business landscape, the ability to anticipate, prepare for, and navigate potential challenges is what separates great leaders from the rest.

Risk management is the process of identifying, assessing, and controlling threats to your organization's capital and earnings. These risks can come from various sources: financial uncertainties, legal liabilities, strategic management errors, accidents, or even natural disasters. Contingency planning, on the other hand, is about preparing for possible future events or circumstances that, while unlikely, could have serious consequences if they do occur.

Let's break down the key components of effective risk management and contingency planning:

1. **Risk Identification:** This involves recognizing and describing potential risks that could affect your project or business. It's about asking "What could go wrong?"
2. **Risk Assessment:** Once risks are identified, you need to analyze their likelihood and potential impact. This helps prioritize which risks need the most attention.
3. **Risk Mitigation:** Develop strategies to reduce the likelihood of risks occurring or to minimize their impact if they do occur.
4. **Contingency Planning:** Create specific action plans for high-priority risks. What exactly will you do if X happens?
5. **Monitoring and Review:** Regularly reassess risks and update your plans. The business environment is always changing, and so should your risk management strategy.

Case Study: The Apollo 13 Mission

One of the most famous examples of successful risk management and contingency planning is NASA's handling of the Apollo 13 mission. When an oxygen tank exploded on board, threatening the lives of the astronauts, NASA's team on the ground had to quickly devise and implement alternative plans to bring the crew home safely.

Key Takeaways:

- Always have backup plans
- Practice problem-solving under pressure
- Maintain clear communication channels
- Prioritize the most critical issues

Discussion Questions:

1. How does NASA's approach to risk management apply to your business or industry?
2. Can you think of a time when your organization faced an unexpected crisis? How was it handled?
3. What potential risks does your organization face? How prepared are you to handle them?

Developing Your Risk Management Skills:

1. **Cultivate a proactive mindset:** Don't wait for problems to occur. Regularly scan your environment for potential risks.
2. **Encourage open communication:** Create an environment where team members feel comfortable reporting potential risks or concerns.
3. **Use scenario planning:** Regularly engage in "what-if" exercises with your team. This helps you prepare for a range of possible futures.
4. **Learn from past experiences:** Conduct post-mortems on both successes and failures to improve future planning.
5. **Stay informed:** Keep up-to-date with industry trends and potential disruptors.
6. **Develop a risk-aware culture:** Integrate risk management into your organization's day-to-day operations.

Activity: Risk Assessment Matrix (15 minutes)

1. Divide participants into small groups.
2. Have each group identify 5-10 potential risks for their organization or a hypothetical business.
3. Create a simple 3x3 matrix with "Likelihood" on one axis (Low, Medium, High) and "Impact" on the other.
4. Place each identified risk in the appropriate cell of the matrix.
5. Discuss which risks should be prioritized based on their position in the matrix.

Remember, the goal of risk management isn't to eliminate all risks - that's impossible. Instead, it's about making informed decisions, being prepared for potential challenges, and positioning your organization to respond effectively when issues arise.

As you go through your week, pay attention to how you and your organization approach risk. Are you being proactive or reactive? Are you prepared for potential challenges? Start thinking about how you can integrate more robust risk management practices into your leadership style.

Reflection Questions:

1. *What's the biggest risk your organization is currently facing? How are you preparing for it?*

2. *Think of a time when you were blindsided by an unexpected problem. How could better risk management have helped?*

3. *How can you create a culture of risk awareness in your team without breeding fear or paralysis?*

Video Break: The Art of Risk Management | Stanley McChrystal (7 min)

[https://www.youtube.com/watch?v=hgcni02chFQ]

Homework:

1. Create a basic risk management plan for your current project or business area. Identify key risks, assess their likelihood and impact, and outline mitigation strategies.
2. Research a major business failure or crisis from the past decade. Analyze what went wrong from a risk management perspective. What lessons can you apply to your own leadership?
3. Schedule a "risk brainstorming" session with your team. Encourage them to think creatively about potential challenges and opportunities.

As we conclude this chapter, remember that effective risk management is not about predicting the future - it's about being prepared for whatever the future might bring. It's about building resilience, adaptability, and a proactive mindset into your leadership and your organization.

In the words of Peter Drucker, *"The best way to predict the future is to create it."* By mastering risk management and contingency planning, you're positioning yourself to create a more secure, successful future for your organization, regardless of what challenges may come your way.

Week 34 - Organizational Alignment (Patrick Lencioni)

"If you could get all the people in an organization rowing in the same direction, you could dominate any industry, in any market, against any competition, at any time." - Patrick Lencioni

In our journey through leadership development, we've explored various aspects of personal excellence and strategic thinking. This week, we turn our attention to a critical element of organizational success: alignment. Patrick Lencioni, renowned author and business consultant, emphasizes the importance of getting everyone in an organization working together towards common goals.

Organizational alignment is about ensuring that every part of your company - from strategy and structure to systems and culture - is in sync and working towards the same objectives. When an organization is aligned, it can achieve remarkable results. Conversely, misalignment can lead to confusion, inefficiency, and ultimately, failure.

Let's explore some key principles of organizational alignment:

1. **Clarity of Purpose:** Everyone in the organization should understand and be committed to the company's mission, vision, and values. This provides a north star for decision-making at all levels.
2. **Strategic Alignment:** Ensure that your strategies, goals, and metrics are all pulling in the same direction. Each department's objectives should clearly contribute to the overall organizational goals.
3. **Structural Alignment:** Your organizational structure should support your strategy. This means having the right roles, reporting relationships, and decision-making processes in place.
4. **Cultural Alignment:** Your company culture should reinforce your strategy and values. This includes the behaviors you reward, the stories you tell, and the way you communicate.
5. **Leadership Alignment:** Your leadership team must be unified in their understanding and communication of the organization's direction. Any misalignment at the top will be amplified throughout the organization.

Lencioni's model of the "Five Dysfunctions of a Team" provides valuable insights into achieving alignment. These dysfunctions are:

1. Absence of Trust
2. Fear of Conflict
3. Lack of Commitment

4. Avoidance of Accountability
5. Inattention to Results

By addressing these dysfunctions, leaders can create a cohesive team that's fully aligned and focused on collective results.

Case Study: Aligning a Tech Startup

Imagine you're the CEO of a rapidly growing tech startup. You've noticed that different departments seem to be working at cross-purposes. The product team is focused on launching new features, while the customer service team is overwhelmed with issues from existing products. The sales team is making promises that the engineering team can't keep up with. How would you approach aligning this organization?

Discussion Questions:

1. What are the key alignment issues in this scenario?
2. How would you use Lencioni's model to address these issues?
3. What specific steps would you take to create better alignment?

Activity: Alignment Audit (15 minutes)

1. Divide participants into small groups.
2. Ask each group to conduct a quick "alignment audit" of their organization or department.

3. Have them identify areas of strong alignment and areas of misalignment.
4. Encourage them to brainstorm specific actions they could take to improve alignment.
5. Have each group share their top insights with the larger group.

Developing Your Alignment Skills:

1. **Practice Clear Communication:** Regularly communicate your organization's mission, vision, and goals. Ensure that everyone understands how their role contributes to these objectives.
2. **Foster Cross-Functional Collaboration:** Create opportunities for different departments to work together and understand each other's challenges and priorities.
3. **Align Incentives:** Ensure that your reward and recognition systems encourage behaviors that support your organizational goals.
4. **Regular Check-ins:** Implement regular meetings or processes to check on alignment and address any emerging issues quickly.
5. **Lead by Example:** As a leader, your actions speak louder than words. Demonstrate alignment in your own decision-making and behavior.

Remember, achieving organizational alignment is an ongoing process, not a one-time event. It requires constant attention, communication, and adjustment. But the rewards - increased efficiency, improved morale, and better results - make it well worth the effort.

Reflection Questions:

1. *How aligned is your current organization or team? What are the signs of alignment or misalignment you observe?*

2. *Think of a time when you were part of a highly aligned team. What made it successful? How did it feel to be part of that team?*

3. *What's one specific action you can take this week to improve alignment in your organization or team?*

More on next page

Video Break: <u>The Importance of Alignment</u> | Patrick Lencioni (8 min)

[https://www.youtube.com/watch?v=wsakqFtjNnE]

As you go through your week, pay attention to signs of alignment and misalignment in your organization. Look for opportunities to foster greater alignment, whether it's clarifying goals, improving communication, or addressing team dysfunctions. Remember, as a leader, you play a crucial role in creating and maintaining organizational alignment. Your ability to get everyone rowing in the same direction can be the difference between mediocrity and excellence.

Homework:

1. Conduct a more detailed alignment audit of your organization or department. Identify specific areas of misalignment and develop an action plan to address them.
2. Read Patrick Lencioni's book "The Advantage: Why Organizational Health Trumps Everything Else in Business" for deeper insights into creating a cohesive, aligned organization.
3. Schedule a meeting with your team to discuss organizational alignment. Use the insights from this chapter to guide your discussion.

By focusing on organizational alignment, you're setting the stage for increased efficiency, better teamwork, and ultimately, greater success. Keep working on aligning your team and organization, and you'll be amazed at what you can achieve together.

Week 35 - Leading Change Initiatives (John Kotter)

"The rate of change is not going to slow down anytime soon. If anything, competition in most industries will probably speed up even more in the next few decades." - John Kotter

As we progress through our leadership journey, we come to a critical skill that every effective leader must master: leading change. In today's rapidly evolving business landscape, the ability to successfully guide your organization through change is not just an asset—it's a necessity.

John Kotter, a renowned expert on leadership and change, has developed an 8-step process for leading change that has become a cornerstone in the field. Let's explore these steps and how you can apply them in your leadership role.

Kotter's 8-Step Process for Leading Change:

1. **Create a Sense of Urgency:** Help others see the need for change and the importance of acting immediately.
2. **Build a Guiding Coalition:** Assemble a group with enough power to lead the change effort.
3. **Form a Strategic Vision and Initiatives:** Create a vision to help direct the change effort and develop strategies for achieving that vision.
4. **Enlist a Volunteer Army:** Communicate the vision and strategies to create buy-in and attract a growing volunteer army of change agents.
5. **Enable Action by Removing Barriers:** Remove obstacles to change, change systems or structures that undermine the vision.
6. **Generate Short-Term Wins:** Plan for and create visible, unambiguous successes as soon as possible.
7. **Sustain Acceleration:** Press harder after the first successes. Be relentless with initiating change after change until the vision is a reality.
8. **Institute Change:** Articulate the connections between new behaviors and organizational success, and develop the means to ensure leadership development and succession.

Case Study: Implementing a New Technology System

Imagine you're the CIO of a large corporation, and you've been tasked with implementing a new enterprise-wide software system. This change will affect every department and require significant adjustments to how people work. How would you approach this change using Kotter's model?

Discussion Questions:

1. How would you create a sense of urgency for this change?
2. Who would you include in your guiding coalition?
3. What potential barriers might you need to remove?
4. How could you generate and celebrate short-term wins during this process?

Developing Your Change Leadership Skills:

1. **Cultivate Emotional Intelligence:** Change can be emotionally challenging for people. Develop your ability to understand and manage emotions—both your own and others'.
2. **Improve Your Communication Skills:** Clear, consistent communication is crucial during change. Practice articulating your vision and the reasons for change in compelling ways.
3. **Build Trust:** Change requires trust. Focus on building and maintaining trust with your team through transparency, consistency, and follow-through.
4. **Develop Resilience:** Change efforts often face setbacks. Work on your ability to bounce back from failures and maintain a positive outlook.
5. **Practice Systems Thinking:** Change in one area often affects others. Develop your ability to see the bigger picture and anticipate ripple effects.

Activity: Change Leadership Simulation (20 minutes)

1. Divide participants into small groups.
2. Present a hypothetical change scenario relevant to your industry.
3. Have each group work through Kotter's 8 steps, developing a brief plan for each step.
4. Ask groups to share their plans, discussing similarities and differences in approaches.

Remember, leading change is not a one-time event but an ongoing process. It requires patience, persistence, and a willingness to adapt your approach as you go. As Kotter says, "Leadership is about coping with change." By mastering these skills, you'll be better equipped to guide your organization through the constant changes of the modern business world.

Reflection Questions:

1. *Think of a significant change you've led or been part of. Which of Kotter's steps were executed well? Which were missing or could have been improved?*

2. *What's your natural reaction to change? How might this impact your ability to lead change?*

3. *What's one specific action you can take this week to improve your change leadership skills?*

As you go through your week, pay attention to changes happening in your organization, no matter how small. Look for opportunities to practice the steps of Kotter's model. Remember, change leadership isn't just for big, organization-wide initiatives—it's a skill you can apply to any situation where you're trying to move from a current state to a desired future state.

Homework:

1. Identify a change initiative in your organization (current or upcoming). Create a brief plan using Kotter's 8 steps.
2. Read John Kotter's book "Leading Change" for a deeper dive into change leadership.
3. Have a conversation with a colleague or mentor about a successful change they've led. What lessons can you apply to your own leadership?

By focusing on developing your change leadership skills, you're preparing yourself to guide your team and organization through the challenges and opportunities of our rapidly evolving world. Remember, effective change leadership isn't about controlling change—it's about facilitating and enabling it. Keep practicing, keep learning, and you'll be well-equipped to lead your team through whatever changes come your way.

Week 36 - Scaling Up Excellence (Robert Sutton)

"The best way to scale is to spread a mindset, not a footprint." - Robert Sutton

As we near the end of our leadership journey, we turn our attention to a critical challenge that many successful leaders face: how to scale up excellence. Whether you're expanding a small team into a larger department, growing a startup into an established company, or spreading best practices across a large organization, the ability to scale excellence is crucial for sustained success.

Robert Sutton, professor at Stanford University and author of *Scaling Up Excellence*, has spent years studying how organizations can spread and sustain their best practices. His research provides valuable insights for leaders looking to scale their success.

Video Break: How to Scale Up Excellence | Dr. Hayagreeva "Huggy" Rao (15 min)

[https://www.youtube.com/watch?v=gk7RfakBZeE]

Key Principles of Scaling Up Excellence:

1. **Spread a mindset, not just a footprint:** Scaling isn't just about growing bigger; it's about spreading a way of thinking and behaving that embodies excellence.
2. **Engage all the senses:** Use multiple channels to communicate and reinforce the desired behaviors and mindsets.
3. **Link short-term realities to long-term dreams:** Help people see how their daily actions connect to the bigger picture.
4. **Accelerate accountability:** As you scale, ensure that people take ownership of their work and its outcomes.
5. **Cut cognitive load:** Simplify processes and eliminate unnecessary complexity to make excellence easier to replicate.
6. **Connect people and cascade excellence:** Foster networks that allow best practices to spread organically.
7. **Eliminate the bad to make way for the good:** Sometimes, scaling up requires first scaling back ineffective practices or behaviors.

Case Study: Scaling Excellence at Pixar

Pixar Animation Studios is renowned for consistently producing high-quality, innovative films. As the company grew from a small team to a large organization, they faced the challenge of maintaining their creative excellence at scale.

Pixar's approach embodied many of Sutton's principles:

1. They spread a mindset of creative risk-taking and continuous improvement.
2. They engaged multiple senses through their collaborative workspace design.
3. They linked short-term work to the long-term vision of creating groundbreaking animated films.
4. They maintained accountability through their "Braintrust" meetings, where frank feedback was encouraged.
5. They simplified their creative process into a repeatable structure, reducing cognitive load.
6. They connected people across departments, allowing ideas to flow freely.
7. They weren't afraid to scrap ideas or even entire projects that weren't meeting their standards of excellence.

Discussion Questions:

1. How does Pixar's approach to scaling excellence apply to your organization or industry?
2. What are some areas of excellence in your organization that could be scaled up?
3. What barriers might you face in scaling up these practices, and how could you overcome them?

Activity: Scaling Up Plan (20 minutes)

1. Identify an area of excellence in your team or organization that you'd like to scale up.
2. Create a plan to scale this excellence using Sutton's principles. Consider:
   - What mindset or behaviors do you need to spread?
   - How can you engage multiple senses in spreading this excellence?
   - How will you link this excellence to your long-term vision?
   - What systems can you put in place to accelerate accountability?
   - How can you simplify processes to reduce cognitive load?
   - How will you connect people to allow excellence to spread?
   - What ineffective practices might you need to eliminate?
3. Share your plan with a partner and provide feedback to each other.

Developing Your Scaling Skills:

1. **Practice systems thinking:** Look at your organization as a whole and understand how different parts interact.
2. **Improve your communication skills:** You'll need to articulate your vision of excellence clearly and compellingly.
3. **Develop your change management skills:** Scaling often involves significant changes, which you'll need to manage effectively.
4. **Foster a culture of continuous learning:** Encourage experimentation and learning from both successes and failures.
5. **Build strong networks:** Cultivate relationships across your organization to help excellence spread organically.

Remember, scaling up excellence is not about achieving perfection everywhere. It's about spreading and sustaining the mindsets and behaviors that drive success. It's an ongoing process that requires patience, persistence, and adaptability.

As you go through your week, pay attention to areas of excellence in your organization. How could these be scaled up? What barriers might you face, and how could you overcome them? Start small, but think big. Every step you take towards scaling excellence brings your organization closer to sustained, widespread success.

Reflection Questions:

1. *What's one area of excellence in your team or organization that you could start scaling up immediately?*

2. *How can you better engage people's hearts and minds in the scaling process?*

3. *What's one specific action you can take this week to start scaling up excellence in your area?*

Homework:

1. Identify an area of excellence in your organization and create a detailed plan to scale it up using Sutton's principles.
2. Read Robert Sutton's book "Scaling Up Excellence" for deeper insights into this crucial leadership skill.
3. Have a conversation with a colleague about how you can collaborate to scale up excellence across departments or teams.

As we conclude this chapter, remember that scaling up excellence is not a one-time event, but an ongoing journey. It requires consistent effort, clear communication, and a willingness to adapt as you learn. But the rewards - a more effective, successful, and impactful organization - are well worth the effort. Keep pushing to spread and sustain excellence, and watch as your leadership impact grows exponentially.

Part 4:

Entrepreneurship and Innovation

Week 37 - Entrepreneurial Mindset (Seth Godin)

"The job isn't to catch up to the status quo; the job is to invent the status quo." - Seth Godin

As we continue our leadership journey, we turn our attention to a critical mindset that can elevate your leadership to new heights: the entrepreneurial mindset. Seth Godin, a renowned entrepreneur, author, and thought leader, has long championed the importance of thinking like an entrepreneur, regardless of your role or industry.

The entrepreneurial mindset isn't just for startup founders or small business owners. It's a powerful approach to leadership that can drive innovation, create value, and navigate uncertainty in any organization. At its core, the entrepreneurial mindset is about seeing opportunities where others see obstacles, taking calculated risks, and being willing to challenge the status quo.

Key Principles of the Entrepreneurial Mindset:

1. **Embrace uncertainty and change:** Entrepreneurs thrive in ambiguity. They see change not as a threat, but as an opportunity to create something new.
2. **Focus on creating value:** Entrepreneurs are obsessed with solving problems and meeting needs in innovative ways. They constantly ask, "How can I add more value?"
3. **Take calculated risks:** Entrepreneurial leaders aren't reckless, but they're not afraid to take smart risks in pursuit of their vision.
4. **Think differently:** Entrepreneurs challenge assumptions and look for new ways of doing things. They're not bound by "the way it's always been done."
5. **Be proactive**: Entrepreneurs don't wait for permission or for conditions to be perfect. They take initiative and make things happen.
6. **Continuously learn and adapt:** The entrepreneurial mindset is one of constant growth and evolution. They see failures as learning opportunities.
7. **Build and leverage networks:** Entrepreneurs understand the power of connections. They build diverse networks and aren't afraid to ask for help or collaborate.

Case Study: Intrapreneurship at 3M

Consider the story of Art Fry at 3M. In the 1970s, Fry was a product development researcher who sang in his church choir. He was frustrated that the small pieces of paper he used to mark pages in his hymnal kept falling out. Remembering a "low-tack" adhesive developed by a colleague, Fry saw an opportunity. He experimented with applying the adhesive to paper, eventually creating what we now know as the Post-it Note.

What's remarkable about this story is not just the invention itself, but how 3M's culture of "intrapreneurship" allowed it to happen. The company gave employees time to work on pet projects and encouraged them to think creatively about solving problems. Fry's entrepreneurial mindset, combined with 3M's supportive culture, led to a product that has generated billions in revenue.

Discussion Questions:

1. How can you foster an entrepreneurial mindset within your team or organization?
2. What barriers might you face in thinking more entrepreneurially in your current role? How can you overcome these?
3. Think of a recent challenge you faced. How might approaching it with an entrepreneurial mindset have changed your approach or the outcome?

Developing Your Entrepreneurial Mindset:

1. **Practice spotting opportunities:** Train yourself to look for unmet needs or inefficiencies in your daily work. Ask, "What could be improved here?"
2. **Cultivate curiosity:** Stay curious about your industry, your customers, and the world at large. Read widely, ask questions, and never stop learning.
3. **Embrace calculated risk-taking:** Start small. Look for low-risk ways to test new ideas or approaches in your work.
4. **Foster a culture of innovation:** Encourage your team to think creatively and share ideas. Create safe spaces for brainstorming and experimentation.

5. **Build diverse networks:** Connect with people outside your immediate circle. Diverse perspectives can spark new ideas and opportunities.

Activity: Entrepreneurial Problem-Solving (20 minutes)

1. Divide into small groups, or as singles.
2. Present each group with a common business challenge
   a. declining customer engagement
   b. inefficient processes
   c. Internal infighting
   d. etc.
3. Ask them to brainstorm innovative solutions using entrepreneurial thinking.
4. Have singles/groups present their ideas to the larger group for feedback.

Remember, developing an entrepreneurial mindset is an ongoing process. It requires practice, persistence, and a willingness to step out of your comfort zone. But the rewards – in terms of innovation, adaptability, and leadership impact – are immense.

As you go through your week, look for opportunities to think and act more entrepreneurially. Challenge assumptions, take calculated risks, and encourage your team to do the same. The entrepreneurial mindset is about seeing possibilities where others see problems, and having the courage to act on those insights.

Reflection Questions:

1. *What's one area in your leadership or organization where you could apply more entrepreneurial thinking?*

2. *How can you better embrace uncertainty and calculated risk-taking in your role?*

3. *What's one specific action you can take this week to start cultivating a more entrepreneurial mindset?*

Homework:

1. Identify a challenge in your organization and develop an innovative, entrepreneurial approach to addressing it.
2. Read Seth Godin's book "Poke the Box" for deeper insights into initiating projects and taking risks.
3. Have a conversation with an entrepreneur or innovative leader about their mindset and approach to problem-solving.

As we conclude this chapter, remember that the entrepreneurial mindset isn't just about starting businesses – it's about starting movements, creating change, and making a meaningful impact. It's about seeing the world not just as it is, but as it could be. By cultivating this mindset, you're positioning yourself to be not just a manager, but a true leader – one who can navigate uncertainty, drive innovation, and create lasting value in whatever role you find yourself.

Embrace the entrepreneurial mindset, and watch as it transforms not just your leadership, but your entire approach to work and life. The world needs more leaders who think like entrepreneurs – who are willing to challenge the status quo, take smart risks, and create the future. Will you be one of them?

Week 38 - Lean Startup Principles (Eric Ries)

"The only way to win is to learn faster than anyone else." - Eric Ries

As we continue our leadership journey, we turn our attention to a methodology that has revolutionized the way businesses approach innovation and growth: the Lean Startup. Developed by Eric Ries, this approach offers valuable insights for leaders in any organization, not just startups.

At its core, the Lean Startup methodology is about reducing waste and increasing efficiency in the process of bringing a new product or service to market. It emphasizes rapid experimentation, customer feedback, and iterative design. While originally conceived for new ventures, these principles can be applied in any context where uncertainty is high and rapid learning is crucial.

Let's explore the key principles of the Lean Startup:

1. **Build-Measure-Learn feedback loop:** This is the fundamental cycle of the Lean Startup. You build a minimum viable product (MVP), measure its effectiveness, and learn from the results. Then you use those learnings to inform your next iteration.
2. **Minimum Viable Product (MVP):** This is a version of a new product that allows a team to collect the maximum amount of validated learning about customers with the least effort. It's about getting your idea in front of customers as quickly as possible to start learning.
3. **Validated learning:** This is the process of demonstrating empirically that a team has discovered valuable truths about a startup's present and future business prospects.
4. **Innovation accounting:** This involves focusing on the boring stuff: how to measure progress, how to set up milestones, and how to prioritize work. It's about holding innovators accountable.
5. **Pivot or persevere:** Based on the validated learning from your MVP, you decide whether to pivot (make a fundamental change to your product or strategy) or persevere (continue on your current path).

Case Study: Dropbox

Consider the story of Dropbox, a file hosting service that has become ubiquitous in our digital lives. When Drew Houston, the founder, first had the idea for Dropbox, he could have spent months or years building a perfect product before launching. Instead, he created a simple video demonstrating how Dropbox would work and posted it on Hacker News.

This video served as an MVP. It allowed Houston to gauge interest in his product without writing a single line of code for the actual service. The response was overwhelming, with thousands of people signing up for the beta waiting list. This validated Houston's assumption that there was a market need for his product.

From there, Dropbox continued to use Lean Startup principles, releasing early versions to users, gathering feedback, and iterating rapidly. They focused on core features that users really needed, rather than trying to build every possible feature from the start.

Discussion Questions:

1. How could you apply the Build-Measure-Learn loop to a current project or challenge in your organization?
2. Think about a recent initiative that didn't go as planned. How might using an MVP approach have changed the outcome?
3. How can you create a culture of experimentation and rapid learning in your team?

Developing Your Lean Leadership Skills:

1. **Practice rapid prototyping:** Get comfortable with releasing "imperfect" versions of your ideas to get feedback. Remember, done is better than perfect.
2. **Cultivate a culture of experimentation:** Encourage your team to test hypotheses and learn from failures. Celebrate learning, not just successes.
3. **Develop your data analysis skills:** Lean Startup relies heavily on measuring and analyzing results. Improve your ability to interpret data and make data-driven decisions.
4. **Foster cross-functional collaboration:** Lean Startup works best when different parts of the organization work closely together. Break down silos and encourage collaboration.

5. **Learn to balance vision and adaptability:** As a leader, you need to maintain a clear vision while being willing to pivot based on what you learn.

Activity: MVP Design Challenge (20 minutes)

1. Divide into small groups/singles.
2. Present each group with a hypothetical product or service idea.
3. Ask them to design an MVP and outline how they would test it.
4. Have groups present their MVPs to the larger group for feedback.

Remember, adopting Lean Startup principles isn't about blindly following a set of rules. It's about embracing a mindset of continuous learning and improvement. It's about being willing to challenge your assumptions and adapt based on real-world feedback.

As you go through your week, look for opportunities to apply these principles in your leadership. Where can you experiment more? How can you get faster feedback on your ideas? How can you measure the impact of your initiatives more effectively?

Reflection Questions:

1. *What's one area in your leadership or organization where you could apply Lean Startup principles?*

2. *How can you better embrace experimentation and validated learning in your role?*

3. *What's one specific action you can take this week to start implementing Lean Startup thinking?*

Homework:

1. Identify a current project or challenge and design an MVP to test a key assumption.
2. Read Eric Ries' book "The Lean Startup" for deeper insights into this methodology.
3. Have a conversation with a colleague about how you can incorporate more rapid experimentation and learning in your work.

As we conclude this chapter, remember that the Lean Startup methodology is about more than just efficiency or rapid growth. It's about creating a culture of innovation, where ideas can be tested quickly and learning is continuous. By adopting these principles, you can lead your team to be more agile, responsive, and innovative in today's fast-paced business environment.

In the words of Eric Ries, *"The big question of our time is not CAN it be built? But SHOULD it be built?"* As a leader, your role is to guide your team in answering that question, using data, experimentation, and rapid learning. Embrace the Lean Startup mindset, and watch as it transforms not just your projects, but your entire approach to leadership and innovation.

Week 39 - Business Model Generation (Alexander Osterwalder)

"A business model describes the rationale of how an organization creates, delivers, and captures value." - Alexander Osterwalder

In our journey through entrepreneurship and innovation, we now turn our attention to a fundamental concept that underpins every successful business: the business model. To guide us in this exploration, we'll draw on the groundbreaking work of Alexander Osterwalder, particularly his Business Model Canvas.

The Business Model Canvas is a strategic management tool that allows you to describe, design, challenge, and pivot your business model. It provides a visual chart with elements describing a firm's value proposition, infrastructure, customers, and finances, offering a holistic view of a business's key drivers.

Let's dive into the nine building blocks of the Business Model Canvas:

1. **Customer Segments:** Who are your most important customers?
2. **Value Propositions:** What value do you deliver to the customer?
3. **Channels:** Through which channels do your customer segments want to be reached?
4. **Customer Relationships:** What type of relationship does each customer segment expect you to establish?
5. **Revenue Streams:** For what value are your customers willing to pay?
6. **Key Resources:** What key resources does your value proposition require?
7. **Key Activities:** What key activities does your value proposition require?
8. **Key Partnerships:** Who are your key partners and suppliers?
9. **Cost Structure:** What are the most important costs inherent in your business model?

These nine blocks work together to provide a comprehensive picture of how a business creates and captures value.

Case Study: Airbnb's Business Model Canvas

Let's examine how this plays out in practice by looking at Airbnb's business model:

- Customer Segments: Travelers seeking unique, affordable accommodations; Property owners looking to earn extra income

- Value Propositions: For travelers - unique stays, local experiences, affordability. For hosts - easy income, meeting new people
- Channels: Website, mobile app, social media, word of mouth
- Customer Relationships: Self-service platform, community, customer support
- Revenue Streams: Service fees from bookings (both guests and hosts)
- Key Resources: Platform technology, user base, brand
- Key Activities: Platform development and maintenance, marketing, customer service
- Key Partnerships: Payment processors, photographers, local experiences providers
- Cost Structure: Technology development, marketing, customer support

This canvas illustrates how Airbnb created a two-sided marketplace, connecting travelers with property owners in a way that creates value for both parties.

Exercise: Creating Your Business Model Canvas

Take a moment to sketch out a Business Model Canvas for your own business or a business idea you're considering. Don't worry about getting it perfect - the canvas is a tool for exploration and iteration.

As you fill out each block, consider:

- How does this element contribute to your overall value proposition?
- How does it interact with the other elements of the canvas?
- What assumptions are you making that might need testing?

Business Model Innovation

Understanding your current business model is just the first step. The real power of the Business Model Canvas lies in its ability to facilitate innovation. By systematically challenging each component of your business model, you can uncover new opportunities for creating and capturing value.

Consider how Netflix disrupted the video rental industry not just through technology, but through business model innovation. They shifted from a pay-per-rental model to a subscription model, fundamentally changing how value was delivered to customers and captured by the company.

Exercise: Business Model Innovation

Looking at your canvas, ask yourself:

- What if we changed our revenue model?
- Could we reach our customers through different channels?
- Is there a way to leverage our key resources to serve new customer segments?

Try to come up with at least three potential innovations to your business model.

Implementing the Business Model Canvas

To get the most out of the Business Model Canvas:

1. **Use it as a team:** The canvas is a powerful tool for aligning your team around a shared understanding of your business model.
2. **Test your assumptions:** Each element of your canvas represents a hypothesis. Find ways to test these hypotheses in the market.
3. **Iterate:** Your business model isn't set in stone. Use the canvas as a dynamic tool, updating it as you learn and grow.
4. **Compare alternatives:** Use multiple canvases to compare different business model options.
5. **Use it for competitive analysis:** Fill out canvases for your competitors to understand their business models and identify opportunities for differentiation.

As you go through your entrepreneurial journey, keep the Business Model Canvas close at hand. Use it not just as a planning tool, but as a dynamic framework for ongoing business model innovation.

Reflection Questions:

1. *How might using the Business Model Canvas change your approach to business planning and strategy?*

2. *Think of a successful company in your industry. How might you fill out their Business Model Canvas? What insights does this give you about their success?*

3. *What's one specific way you could innovate your business model in the next month?*

Remember, as Osterwalder says, *"Your business model is nothing else than your strategy made explicit."* By mastering the art of business model generation, we equip ourselves to create, deliver, and capture value in innovative and sustainable ways. This is the essence of entrepreneurship and the key to long-term business success.

Week 40 - Blue Ocean Strategy (Renée Mauborgne)

"The best way to beat the competition is to stop trying to beat the competition." - W. Chan Kim and Renée Mauborgne

In our previous chapter, we explored the art of business model generation. Now, we turn our attention to a revolutionary approach to strategy that has transformed industries and created unprecedented value: Blue Ocean Strategy. Developed by W. Chan Kim and Renée Mauborgne, this approach challenges us to break out of the bloody "red oceans" of existing market space and create uncontested "blue oceans" of new market opportunities.

The Concept of Blue Ocean Strategy

At its core, Blue Ocean Strategy is about creating and capturing new demand, rather than fighting over existing customers. It's about making the competition irrelevant by creating a leap in value for both the company and its customers.

Kim and Mauborgne use the metaphor of red and blue oceans to describe the market universe:

- **Red Oceans are all the industries in existence today** - the known market space. In red oceans, industry boundaries are defined and accepted, and the competitive rules of the game are known.
- **Blue Oceans, in contrast, are defined by untapped market space**, demand creation, and the opportunity for highly profitable growth. In blue oceans, competition is irrelevant because the rules of the game are waiting to be set.

The Four Actions Framework

To create blue oceans, Kim and Mauborgne propose the Four Actions Framework:

1. **Eliminate:** Which factors that the industry has long competed on should be eliminated?
2. **Reduce:** Which factors should be reduced well below the industry's standard?
3. **Raise:** Which factors should be raised well above the industry's standard?
4. **Create:** Which factors should be created that the industry has never offered?

This framework pushes us to simultaneously pursue differentiation and low cost, breaking the value-cost trade-off that traditionally defines strategy.

Case Study: Cirque du Soleil

Let's examine how Cirque du Soleil applied Blue Ocean Strategy to reinvent the circus industry:

- Eliminated: Star performers, animal shows, multiple show arenas
- Reduced: Fun and humor, thrills and danger
- Raised: Unique venue, artistic music and dance, multiple productions
- Created: Theme, refined watching environment, artistic music and dance

By eliminating or reducing the most expensive elements of the circus and raising factors that appealed to a new audience, Cirque du Soleil created a new form of entertainment that drew from both theater and circus traditions. They didn't compete in the existing circus market; they created a new market space that appealed to a whole new group of customers willing to pay a premium for a novel entertainment experience.

Exercise: The Strategy Canvas

The Strategy Canvas is a key analytical tool in Blue Ocean Strategy. It captures the current state of play in the known market space, allowing you to understand where the competition is currently investing and the factors the industry currently competes on.

Take a moment to create a Strategy Canvas for your industry:

1. List the key competing factors along the horizontal axis
2. Plot the offering level that buyers receive across these key competing factors
3. Draw the "value curve" - the graphic depiction of a company's relative performance across its industry's factors of competition

Now, consider:

- Where is everyone in your industry clustered?
- Where could you diverge to create unique value?

Creating Your Blue Ocean Strategy

To create your own Blue Ocean Strategy:

1. Identify which factors to eliminate, reduce, raise, and create using the Four Actions Framework
2. Reconstruct market boundaries by:
    - Looking across alternative industries
    - Looking across strategic groups within industries
    - Looking across the chain of buyers
    - Looking across complementary product and service offerings
    - Looking across functional or emotional appeal to buyers
    - Looking across time
3. Focus on the big picture, not the numbers
4. Reach beyond existing demand
5. Get the strategic sequence right: utility, price, cost, adoption

Exercise: Blue Ocean Opportunity

Think about your own business or industry:

- What factors could you eliminate that others take for granted?
- What could you reduce far below the industry standard?
- What could you raise far above the industry standard?
- What could you create that the industry has never offered?

Write down your ideas and consider how they might come together to create a leap in value for your customers and your business.

Implementing Blue Ocean Strategy

Implementing a Blue Ocean Strategy isn't without challenges. You may face organizational hurdles, resource limitations, and motivational challenges. To overcome these:

1. **Build execution into strategy:** Involve key stakeholders in the strategy creation process

2. **Overcome key organizational hurdles:** Address cognitive, resource, motivational, and political hurdles head-on
3. **Build your people's confidence:** Break the change process into achievable steps

Remember, creating blue oceans is not a static achievement but a dynamic process. Even the most powerful blue ocean strategy will eventually be imitated. Thus, companies need to monitor their value curves constantly and be ready to create new blue oceans when existing ones become crowded.

Reflection Questions:

1. *How might adopting a Blue Ocean Strategy mindset change your approach to competition and innovation?*

2. *Think of a successful company that created a blue ocean. What can you learn from their approach?*

3. *What's one specific way you could start exploring blue ocean opportunities in your business in the next month?*

As we continue our entrepreneurial journey, let's remember that true innovation often comes not from outcompeting others, but from making competition irrelevant. By mastering the principles of Blue Ocean Strategy, we equip ourselves to create new market space, unlock new demand, and achieve both differentiation and low cost. This is the path to sustainable, profitable growth in an increasingly competitive world.

Week 41 - Disruptive Innovation (Clayton Christensen)

"The reason why it is so difficult for existing firms to capitalize on disruptive innovations is that their processes and their business model that make them good at the existing business actually make them bad at competing for the disruption." - Clayton Christensen

In our previous chapter, we explored the concept of Blue Ocean Strategy and creating uncontested market space. Now, we turn our attention to a powerful force that has reshaped industries and toppled market leaders: Disruptive Innovation. This concept, introduced by Harvard Business School professor Clayton Christensen, has become a cornerstone of modern innovation theory and practice.

Understanding Disruptive Innovation

At its core, disruptive innovation describes a process by which a product or service initially takes root in simple applications at the bottom of a market—typically by being less expensive and more accessible—and then relentlessly moves upmarket, eventually displacing established competitors.

Christensen distinguishes between two types of innovations:

1. **Sustaining Innovations:** These improve existing products along the dimensions historically valued by customers. Most innovations fall into this category.
2. **Disruptive Innovations:** These create an entirely new market through the introduction of a new kind of product or service, one that's actually worse, initially, as judged by the performance metrics that mainstream customers value.

The Innovator's Dilemma

One of Christensen's key insights is that the very things that make established companies successful in their current markets make it extremely difficult for them to develop and nurture disruptive innovations. This is known as the innovator's dilemma.

Established companies focus on sustaining innovations because that's what their mainstream customers demand. They're motivated to move upmarket to improve profit margins. However, this leaves them vulnerable to disruptors who enter at the bottom of the market with lower-performance but "good enough" products that appeal to overlooked customers or entirely new markets.

Case Study: Netflix vs. Blockbuster

Consider the classic example of Netflix disrupting Blockbuster:

- Initially, Netflix offered a DVD-by-mail service, which was less convenient in some ways than Blockbuster's stores (you couldn't get a movie immediately).
- However, it appealed to movie buffs who wanted a wider selection and didn't mind waiting.
- As Netflix improved its service and introduced streaming, it moved upmarket, eventually displacing Blockbuster entirely.

Blockbuster, focused on its mainstream customers and high-margin late fees, failed to respond effectively to this disruptive threat until it was too late.

Exercise: Identifying Disruptive Threats and Opportunities

Think about your own industry:

1. What potential disruptive threats exist? Are there any low-end competitors or new market entrants that established players are ignoring?
2. What disruptive opportunities could you pursue? Are there overlooked customer segments or "non-consumers" you could serve with a "good enough" solution?

Write down your ideas and consider how they might evolve to reshape your industry.

Jobs to Be Done Theory

Another key concept in Christensen's work is the Jobs to Be Done (JTBD) theory. This approach suggests that customers don't buy products or services; they "hire" them to do a specific job.

Understanding the job that customers are trying to get done provides much deeper insight than traditional market segmentation. It helps innovators create products that customers really want.

Exercise: Jobs to Be Done Analysis

Choose a product or service your company offers (or one you use regularly):

1. What job is the customer hiring this product to do?
2. What are the functional aspects of this job?
3. What are the emotional and social dimensions of this job?
4. Are there aspects of the job that aren't being satisfied by current solutions?

This analysis can reveal opportunities for both sustaining and disruptive innovations.

Strategies for Dealing with Disruptive Innovation

For established companies facing disruptive threats, Christensen suggests several strategies:

1. Create a separate division to pursue disruptive innovations
2. Acquire a disruptive innovator
3. Be the disruptor by cannibalizing your own market before others do

For entrepreneurs and innovators looking to create disruptive innovations:

1. Look for jobs that aren't being done well by existing solutions
2. Start with a low-end or new-market foothold
3. Don't chase large, established markets immediately - be patient for growth but impatient for profitability
4. Be prepared for resistance from established players

Implementing Disruptive Innovation

To foster disruptive innovation in your organization:

1. Create a culture that embraces risk and isn't afraid to cannibalize existing products
2. Allocate resources to exploring potentially disruptive ideas, even if they don't seem profitable initially
3. Use the Jobs to Be Done framework to deeply understand customer needs
4. Be willing to start small and move upmarket over time
5. Continuously scan the market for potential disruptors, especially at the low end

Remember, disruptive innovation is not about creating breakthrough technologies, but about business models that can take those technologies to a broad, new market.

Reflection Questions:

1. *How might adopting a disruptive innovation mindset change your approach to product development and market strategy?*

2. *Think of a successful disruptive innovator. What can you learn from their approach?*

3. *What's one specific way you could start exploring disruptive opportunities or addressing disruptive threats in your business in the next month?*

As we continue our entrepreneurial journey, let's remember that true innovation often comes not from doing things better, but from doing things differently. By understanding and applying the principles of disruptive innovation, we equip ourselves to create new markets, serve overlooked customers, and build businesses that can thrive in an era of constant change and disruption.

Week 42 - Design Thinking (Tim Brown)

"Design thinking is a human-centered approach to innovation that draws from the designer's toolkit to integrate the needs of people, the possibilities of technology, and the requirements for business success." - Tim Brown

In our previous chapter, we explored the disruptive power of innovation. Now, we turn our attention to a methodology that has revolutionized the way companies approach problem-solving and innovation: Design Thinking. Popularized by IDEO and its CEO Tim Brown, Design Thinking is a human-centered approach to innovation that integrates empathy, creativity, and rationality to meet user needs and drive business success.

Understanding Design Thinking

At its core, Design Thinking is about understanding the people for whom we're designing products or services. It's a methodology that helps us step back from our assumptions and approach problems with fresh eyes, always keeping the end-user at the center of our process.

The Design Thinking process consists of five key stages:

1. **Empathize:** Understand the user's needs, thoughts, feelings, and motivations.
2. **Define:** Clearly articulate the problem you're trying to solve based on user insights.
3. **Ideate:** Generate a wide range of creative ideas.
4. **Prototype:** Build quick, low-fidelity representations of your ideas.
5. **Test:** Get feedback from your users and refine your solutions.

It's important to note that these stages are not always sequential. Design Thinking is an iterative process, and you may find yourself moving back and forth between stages as you gain new insights.

The Power of Empathy

The first and perhaps most crucial stage of Design Thinking is empathy. This involves setting aside our own assumptions and truly understanding the user's perspective.

Exercise: Empathy Mapping

Think about a product or service you're working on. Now, consider your target user and create an empathy map:

- What does the user think and feel?
- What does the user see in their environment?
- What does the user hear from friends, family, and influencers?
- What does the user say and do publicly?

This exercise helps us step into our users' shoes and understand their world, which is crucial for designing solutions that truly meet their needs.

Defining the Problem

Once we have a deep understanding of our users, we can more accurately define the problem we're trying to solve. A well-defined problem statement sets the stage for innovative solutions.

In Design Thinking, we often frame problem statements as "How Might We" questions. For example, instead of "Our app is difficult to navigate," we might ask, "How might we create a more intuitive navigation experience for our users?"

Exercise: Problem Definition

Based on your empathy map, try to define the core problem your user is facing. Frame it as a "How Might We" question.

Remember, the goal is to define the problem in a way that invites creative solutions.

Ideation: Generating Creative Solutions

With a clear problem statement, we can now generate a wide range of potential solutions. The key here is quantity over quality - we want to create a large pool of ideas from which we can later select the most promising ones.

There are many techniques for ideation, including:

- **Brainstorming:** Generate as many ideas as possible without judgment.
- **Mind Mapping:** Visually organize information and explore connections.
- **SCAMPER:** Use prompts (Substitute, Combine, Adapt, Modify, Put to another use, Eliminate, Reverse) to generate new ideas.

Remember, in the ideation phase, there are no bad ideas. Wild ideas often lead to innovative breakthroughs.

Prototyping and Testing

In Design Thinking, we believe in "thinking with our hands." Prototyping allows us to quickly and cheaply bring our ideas to life so we can test them with users.

Prototypes don't need to be perfect or fully functional. They can be as simple as a paper sketch or a role-playing exercise. The goal is to create something tangible that users can interact with and provide feedback on.

Testing is where we bring our prototypes to users and gather their feedback. This stage often leads us back to earlier stages as we gain new insights about our users and refine our understanding of the problem.

Case Study: Airbnb's $30 Billion Insight

Airbnb provides a great example of Design Thinking in action. In the early days of the company, bookings were flat. The founders decided to fly to New York, their biggest market, to figure out why.

They visited hosts and looked at their listings. They realized that the photos on the site were poor quality, making spaces look unappealing. Their "prototype" was simple: they rented a high-end camera and took better photos of the listings themselves.

A week later, the New York listings with improved photos saw two to three times more bookings. This simple, user-centered solution led to a significant turning point for the company.

Implementing Design Thinking

To foster Design Thinking in your organization:

1. **Encourage empathy:** Create opportunities for team members to directly interact with and observe users.
2. **Embrace ambiguity:** Be comfortable with not knowing the answer right away.
3. Foster a culture of experimentation: Encourage quick prototyping and learning from failure.
4. **Promote cross-functional collaboration:** Diverse perspectives lead to more innovative solutions.
5. **Make it tangible:** Use visuals, prototypes, and storytelling to communicate ideas.

Remember, Design Thinking is not a linear process. It's a mindset that encourages continuous learning and refinement based on user feedback.

Reflection Questions:

1. *How might adopting a Design Thinking approach change the way you develop products or services?*

2. *Think of a successful product or service. How do you think empathy for the user contributed to its success?*

3. *What's one specific way you could incorporate more user empathy into your current projects?*

As we continue our journey in innovation and entrepreneurship, let's remember that the most successful solutions are those that truly understand and meet user needs. By mastering

Design Thinking, we equip ourselves to create products and services that not only solve problems but also resonate deeply with our users, leading to greater adoption, satisfaction, and business success.

Week 43 - Jobs To Be Done Theory (Clayton Christensen)

"People don't want to buy a quarter-inch drill. They want a quarter-inch hole."

- Theodore Levitt

In our previous chapter, we explored the transformative power of Design Thinking. Now, we turn our attention to another revolutionary framework that has changed how businesses understand customer needs: Jobs To Be Done (JTBD) theory. Popularized by Clayton Christensen and further developed by innovators like Bob Moesta and Tony Ulwick, this approach provides a powerful lens for understanding why customers "hire" products and services.

Understanding Jobs To Be Done Theory

At its core, JTBD theory suggests that customers don't buy products or services; they "hire" them to get jobs done in their lives. These jobs represent the progress that customers are trying to make in particular circumstances.

<u>For example:</u>

- People don't just buy milkshakes; they hire them to make a boring commute more interesting and to stave off hunger until lunchtime.
- People don't just buy mattresses; they hire them to provide a good night's sleep and to avoid disturbing their partners when they move.
- People don't just buy accounting software; they hire it to stay compliant with tax laws and to understand their financial position.

This shift in perspective—from focusing on the product itself to understanding the job it's hired to do—opens up new avenues for innovation and customer understanding.

The Three Dimensions of Jobs

Jobs typically have three dimensions:

1. **Functional dimension:** The practical task the customer wants to accomplish.
2. **Emotional dimension:** How the customer wants to feel or avoid feeling.
3. **Social dimension:** How the customer wants to be perceived by others.

For example, when someone "hires" a luxury watch, the functional job might be to tell time, but the emotional job might be to feel successful, and the social job might be to be perceived as sophisticated or accomplished.

Exercise: Identifying Jobs for Your Product

Think about a product or service your company offers. What jobs are customers hiring it to do? Consider all three dimensions:

What functional jobs is it performing?
What emotional jobs is it performing?
What social jobs is it performing?

Write down as many jobs as you can think of. Then, consider whether your product is optimally designed to perform these jobs, or if there are opportunities to better align your offering with customer needs.

_____

_____

_____

_____

The "Job Interview"

To uncover the jobs your customers are hiring your product to do, consider conducting "job interviews." Unlike traditional market research that focuses on demographics or feature preferences, a job interview aims to understand the circumstances and motivations that led customers to "hire" your product.

Key questions in a job interview might include:

1. What were you trying to accomplish when you decided to use our product?
2. What solutions had you tried before?
3. What made you decide to switch?
4. What would you be doing if our product didn't exist?
5. What obstacles almost prevented you from using our product?

These questions help reveal not just what customers are using your product for, but why they chose it over alternatives, including doing nothing at all.

Case Study: Competing Against "Nothing"

Consider the case of a company that sold hospital equipment. They were losing deals and couldn't figure out why their technically superior product wasn't winning. Through JTBD interviews, they discovered that many hospitals were choosing to do nothing rather than buy new equipment.

The job wasn't just about having better equipment; it was about minimizing disruption to existing workflows and avoiding the need for additional training. By understanding this, the company was able to redesign their offering to include comprehensive training and implementation support, addressing the real job hospitals needed done.

This illustrates a key insight from JTBD theory: You're often competing against "nothing" or "the current way of doing things," not just other products in your category.

For your product or service, ask:

- ❖ What are customers doing now to get the job done?
- ❖ What happens if they do nothing?
- ❖ What other solutions (even in different categories) might they consider?

This broader view of competition can reveal unexpected threats and opportunities.

Implementing Jobs Theory in Your Business

To apply *Jobs To Be Done* theory effectively:

1. **Focus on circumstances, not characteristics:** Understand the situations that trigger the need for your product, not just who your customers are.

2. **Look for workarounds:** Pay attention to how customers are cobbling together solutions or adapting existing products to get jobs done.

3. **Study switching behavior:** The moment when customers switch from one solution to another provides rich insights into the real job they're trying to get done.

4. **Embrace the "why behind the why":** Keep asking why until you uncover the fundamental job.

5. **Design around the job, not just the customer:** Organize your innovation efforts around solving specific jobs better than current alternatives.

Reflection Questions:

1. *How might adopting a Jobs To Be Done perspective change your approach to product development or marketing?*

2. *Think of a successful product or service. What job is it being hired to do? How does its design and marketing align with that job?*

3. *What's one specific way you could incorporate Jobs To Be Done theory into your current business practices?*

As we continue our entrepreneurial journey, let's remember that understanding the true jobs our customers are hiring our products to do is the key to creating offerings that resonate deeply and drive lasting success. By focusing not just on what customers are buying, but why they're buying it, we can innovate in ways that truly matter.

In the words of Clayton Christensen, *"When we buy a product, we essentially 'hire' it to help us do a job. If it does the job well, the next time we're confronted with the same job, we tend to hire that product again. And if it does a crummy job, we 'fire' it and look for an alternative."*

Week 44 - Building Minimum Viable Products

"If you are not embarrassed by the first version of your product, you've launched too late."

- Reid Hoffman

In our previous chapter, we explored the Jobs To Be Done theory and how understanding customer motivations can transform our approach to product development. Now, we turn our attention to a critical concept in modern entrepreneurship: the Minimum Viable Product (MVP). This approach, popularized by Eric Ries in his book *The Lean Startup*, has revolutionized how startups and established companies alike bring new products to market.

Understanding the Minimum Viable Product

An MVP is the version of a new product that allows a team to collect the maximum amount of validated learning about customers with the least effort. Contrary to common misconception, an MVP is not simply a stripped-down version of your product. Rather, it's a strategic approach to product development that emphasizes learning and iteration.

The key principles behind an effective MVP are:

1. **Focus on learning:** The primary goal is to test your fundamental business hypotheses, not to create a perfect product.
2. **Minimum effort:** Invest only what's necessary to validate your key assumptions.
3. **Viable:** Despite being minimal, it must deliver enough value to attract early adopters.
4. **Product:** It's something customers can actually use, not just conceptual or theoretical.

Case Study: Dropbox's MVP

Dropbox provides a classic example of an effective MVP. Instead of building their full cloud storage solution immediately, founder Drew Houston created a simple 3-minute video demonstrating how Dropbox would work. This video allowed them to:

1. Validate customer interest without building the actual product
2. Gather email addresses from interested potential users
3. Understand what features were most important to customers

The waitlist grew from 5,000 to 75,000 people overnight, providing strong validation for their concept before they wrote a single line of code for the actual product.

This case illustrates a key insight: an MVP doesn't always have to be a working product. It can be any experiment that helps you validate your core assumptions.

Why Build an MVP?

The traditional product development approach often involves spending significant time and resources building a "perfect" product before getting customer feedback. This approach is risky because:

- ❖ You might build features customers don't want
- ❖ Market conditions might change during development
- ❖ You could run out of resources before launch
- ❖ You miss opportunities to learn and adapt

By contrast, the MVP approach allows you to:

- ❖ Test your core assumptions quickly
- ❖ Get real customer feedback early
- ❖ Allocate resources more efficiently
- ❖ Adapt based on validated learning
- ❖ Reduce the risk of major failure

Exercise: Identifying Your Core Assumptions

Think about a product or service idea you're considering. What are the 3-5 most critical assumptions that must be true for this idea to succeed? These might include:

- ★ Customers have the problem you're trying to solve

- ★ They're willing to pay for a solution
- ★ Your solution is better than existing alternatives
- ★ You can acquire customers cost-effectively

Once you've identified these assumptions, consider what type of MVP would best validate them with minimal resources.

Types of MVPs

MVPs come in many forms, depending on what you need to learn:

1. **Concierge MVP:** Manually deliver your service to a small number of customers to understand their needs (e.g., Airbnb's founders photographing and listing their own apartment).

2. **Wizard of Oz MVP:** Create the illusion of a fully functional product while manually handling operations behind the scenes (e.g., Zappos initially buying shoes from retail stores when customers ordered online).

3. *Landing Page MVP:* Create a website describing your product and measure interest through sign-ups or pre-orders.

4. **Video MVP:** Like Dropbox, create a video demonstrating how your product would work.

5. **Single-Feature MVP:** Build only the core feature that delivers the primary value proposition.

6. **Piecemeal MVP:** Cobble together existing tools and services to deliver your solution.

The right approach depends on what you need to learn, the nature of your product, and the resources available to you.

The Build-Measure-Learn Cycle

The MVP is just the beginning of a continuous process of learning and iteration. The Build-Measure-Learn cycle is at the heart of the Lean Startup methodology:

1. **Build:** Create your MVP based on your current assumptions.
2. **Measure:** Gather data on how customers interact with your MVP.
3. **Learn:** Use that data to validate or invalidate your assumptions.

This cycle then repeats, with each iteration building on what you've learned.

Exercise: Designing Your MVP Experiment

For your product idea:

1. What is the simplest version you could build to test your core assumptions?
2. How will you measure success? What metrics matter most?
3. What will you do with what you learn? How might your idea evolve?

Remember, the goal is not perfection but learning. Your first version should be just good enough to start the conversation with customers.

Implementing the MVP Approach

To effectively implement the MVP approach in your organization:

1. **Embrace a learning mindset:** View your product as a set of hypotheses to be tested, not a vision to be executed.

2. **Define success metrics upfront:** Know what data you need to collect and what would constitute validation.

3. **Talk to customers:** Quantitative data is valuable, but direct customer feedback is equally important.

4. **Be prepared to pivot:** If your assumptions prove wrong, be willing to change direction based on what you learn.

5. **Balance vision and validation:** While being responsive to data, maintain a clear vision of the problem you're solving.

Reflection Questions:

1. *How might adopting an MVP approach change your product development process?*

2. *Think of a successful product. How could it have been simplified to an MVP that still delivered core value?*

3. *What's one product idea you could test with an MVP in the next month?*

As we continue our entrepreneurial journey, let's remember that building successful products isn't about getting everything right the first time. It's about creating a feedback loop that allows us to learn, adapt, and ultimately deliver something that truly meets customer needs.

In the words of Eric Ries, "The only way to win is to learn faster than anyone else." The MVP approach gives us a framework to do just that, minimizing waste while maximizing our chances of creating products that matter.

Week 45 - Pitching and Storytelling (Nancy Duarte)

"Stories are just data with a soul." - Brené Brown

In our previous chapter, we explored the concept of Minimum Viable Products and how they help entrepreneurs validate their ideas with minimal resources. Now, we turn our attention to a critical skill that can make or break a startup's success: the art of pitching and storytelling. Drawing on the wisdom of communication expert Nancy Duarte and other masters of persuasion, we'll explore how to craft narratives that inspire action and drive results.

The Power of Story

Humans are wired for stories. From ancient campfires to modern boardrooms, stories have been our primary means of sharing information, creating connection, and inspiring action. As entrepreneurs and leaders, our ability to craft and deliver compelling narratives can determine whether our ideas gain traction or fade into obscurity.

Why does storytelling matter in business?

1. **Stories make information memorable:** Research shows that information delivered as a story is up to 22 times more memorable than facts alone.

2. **Stories create emotional connection:** They engage not just the logical brain, but also the emotional centers that drive decision-making.

3. **Stories simplify complexity:** They provide a framework that helps audiences make sense of complex ideas.

4. **Stories inspire action:** Well-told stories can move people from understanding to caring to doing.

The Structure of a Compelling Pitch

Nancy Duarte, in her analysis of great presentations, identified a common pattern she calls the "presentation form." Great pitches oscillate between what is (the current reality) and what could be (the envisioned future), creating tension that resolves in a call to action.

This structure follows a basic format:

1. **Start with the status quo:** Establish common ground with your audience by acknowledging the current situation.

2. **Introduce the conflict:** Highlight the gap between the current reality and what could be.

3. **Present your resolution:** Show how your idea bridges this gap.

4. **End with a clear call to action:** Tell your audience exactly what you want them to do.

Exercise: Mapping Your Presentation

Think about a pitch you need to make—whether for a new product, a funding request, or a strategic initiative. Map out:

- ❖ What is the current reality your audience recognizes?
- ❖ What is the better future you envision?
- ❖ How does your idea bridge the gap?
- ❖ What specific action do you want your audience to take?

The Hero's Journey in Business Pitching

Another powerful framework for structuring your pitch is the Hero's Journey, adapted from Joseph Campbell's work on mythology. In business storytelling, there's a crucial twist: your customer, not your company, is the hero.

The structure looks something like this:

1. **The Ordinary World:** Describe the status quo for your customer.

2. **The Call to Adventure:** Introduce the problem or opportunity your customer faces.

3. **Refusal of the Call:** Acknowledge the resistance or challenges that might hold them back.

4. **Meeting the Mentor:** Enter your company or product as the guide that will help them succeed.

5. **Crossing the Threshold:** Show how your solution helps them take the first step.

6. **Tests, Allies, and Enemies:** Address obstacles and how your solution overcomes them.

7. **The Reward:** Highlight the benefits and outcomes of adopting your solution.

8. **The Return:** Describe how their world is transformed by your solution.

Case Study: Steve Jobs and the iPod Pitch

Consider how Steve Jobs announced the original iPod in 2001. Instead of leading with technical specifications, he started with a customer problem: "This amazing little device holds 1,000 songs and it goes right in my pocket."

Jobs made the customer the hero of the story, addressing their desire for music on the go. He didn't sell a device with 5GB of storage; he sold "1,000 songs in your pocket"—transforming technical features into customer benefits.

This approach epitomizes what makes a pitch compelling: it's not about what your product is, but about how it transforms your customer's world.

Know Your Audience

Effective pitching begins with understanding your audience. Before crafting your message, ask:

1. What does my audience already know?
2. What do they care about most?
3. What objections might they have?
4. What outcome would they consider a success?

Tailoring your pitch to address these questions dramatically increases your chances of connecting and persuading.

Exercise: Audience Empathy Map

For your next pitch, create an empathy map for your audience:

- ❖ What are they thinking about?
- ❖ What are they feeling?
- ❖ What are they seeing in their environment?
- ❖ What are they hearing from others?
- ❖ What are their pain points?
- ❖ What are their goals?

Use this understanding to craft a message that resonates with their specific concerns and aspirations.

The Art of Visual Storytelling

Nancy Duarte emphasizes that visual design is not just about aesthetics—it's about clarity and impact. Your slides or visual aids should:

1. Be simple and focused: One idea per slide.
2. Use visuals that enhance understanding, not decorate.
3. Minimize text: Use keywords, not paragraphs.
4. Create visual hierarchy: Guide the eye to what matters most.
5. Use contrast to highlight key points.

Remember, your slides are a backdrop for your story, not the story itself.

Even the most beautifully crafted pitch can fall flat without effective delivery. Consider these elements:

1. **Authenticity:** Be genuine and passionate about your idea.

2. **Confidence:** Practice until you're comfortable with the material.

3. **Connection:** Make eye contact and read the room.

4. **Pacing:** Vary your pace and include strategic pauses.

5. **Body language:** Use purposeful movement and gestures.

6. **Voice modulation:** Vary your tone and volume to emphasize key points.

Exercise: The Elevator Pitch

Craft a 30-second version of your pitch that captures the essence of your idea. This forces you to distill your message to its most compelling core. Practice delivering this elevator pitch until it feels natural and engaging.

_____

_____

_____

_____

_____

Handling Questions and Objections

Questions and objections are not threats but opportunities to deepen understanding and address concerns. Prepare for them by:

1. Anticipating likely questions and preparing concise answers.

2. Embracing the "Yes, and..." approach rather than becoming defensive.

3. Having backup slides or data ready for detailed inquiries.

4. Being honest when you don't know an answer, but offering to follow up.

Remember, how you handle challenging questions often has more impact than your prepared remarks.

Reflection Questions:

1. *Think of a recent pitch or presentation you gave. How might the storytelling principles we've discussed have made it more effective?*

2. *Consider a successful pitch you've witnessed. What elements made it compelling, and how could you incorporate those into your own communication?*

3. *What's one specific way you could improve your pitching and storytelling skills in the next month?*

As we continue our entrepreneurial journey, let's remember that our ideas—no matter how brilliant—will only succeed if we can communicate them effectively to others. By mastering the art of pitching and storytelling, we equip ourselves to inspire, persuade, and ultimately transform our visions into reality.

In the words of Maya Angelou, *"People will forget what you said, people will forget what you did, but people will never forget how you made them feel."* Through powerful storytelling, we can create feelings that drive action and bring our ideas to life.

Week 46 - Negotiation Skills (Chris Voss)

"You don't get what you deserve. You get what you negotiate." - Chester L. Karrass

In our previous chapter, we explored the art of pitching and storytelling. Now, we turn our attention to a critical skill that impacts almost every aspect of business and leadership: negotiation. Drawing on the wisdom of negotiation expert Chris Voss, former FBI hostage negotiator and author of *Never Split the Difference*, along with other negotiation masters, we'll explore how to create value and build relationships through effective negotiation.

Understanding Modern Negotiation

Negotiation has evolved significantly from the old-school "win-lose" approach. Today's most effective negotiators understand that the best outcomes often come from collaborative problem-solving rather than adversarial positioning.

At its core, negotiation is not about defeating the other party—it's about finding solutions that satisfy the underlying interests of all parties involved. As Chris Voss emphasizes, "Negotiation is not an act of battle; it's a process of discovery."

The Three Fundamental Approaches to Negotiation

1. **Positional Bargaining:** The traditional approach where each side takes a position and makes concessions until they meet somewhere in the middle. This often leaves value on the table and can damage relationships.

2. **Interest-Based Negotiation:** Developed at Harvard's Negotiation Project and described in the book "Getting to Yes," this approach focuses on understanding the underlying interests of all parties and finding creative solutions that satisfy those interests.

3. **Tactical Empathy:** Chris Voss's approach, which combines psychological insights with practical techniques to create connection and uncover information that leads to better outcomes.

The most effective negotiators draw from all three approaches, adapting their strategy to the specific situation.

Chris Voss revolutionized negotiation theory by introducing the concept of "tactical empathy"—the deliberate influencing of your counterpart's emotions for the purpose of building rapport, gaining trust, and understanding their position.

Key elements of tactical empathy include:

1. **Active Listening:** Fully focusing on what the other person is saying, rather than planning your response.

2. **Labeling Emotions:** Identifying and acknowledging the emotions the other party is experiencing with phrases like "It seems like..." or "It sounds like..."

3. **Mirroring:** Repeating the last few words or critical phrases the other person said to encourage them to elaborate and feel understood.

4. **Using Calibrated Questions:** Open-ended questions that begin with "How" or "What" to gather information and shift the burden of solution-finding.

Exercise: Practicing Tactical Empathy

Think of a recent or upcoming negotiation. For each party involved:

❖ What are their likely emotional states going into the negotiation?
❖ What labels could you use to acknowledge those emotions?
❖ What calibrated questions could you ask to better understand their perspective?

The Psychology of Negotiation

Understanding the psychological principles at play can give you a significant advantage in negotiations:

1. **Anchoring:** The first number mentioned in a negotiation has a powerful influence on the final outcome. This is why understanding when to make the first offer is crucial.

2. **Loss Aversion:** People feel the pain of losses more acutely than the pleasure of equivalent gains. Framing your proposal in terms of what the other party might lose by not accepting can be powerful.

3. **Reciprocity:** People feel obligated to return favors. Making concessions can trigger reciprocal concessions from your counterpart.

4. **Contrast Principle:** A proposal that might seem expensive in isolation may seem reasonable when presented after a more expensive alternative.

5. **Status Quo Bias:** People tend to prefer the current state. Demonstrating how your proposal minimizes disruption can be effective.

Case Study: The '$1,500 Rule' Negotiation

Consider this example from Chris Voss: A client was negotiating the purchase of a new car. The dealership offered a price that was $1,500 above what the client wanted to pay. Rather than counter with a lower number (positional bargaining), the client used tactical empathy:

Client: "I'm sorry, but $1,500 more is a bit steep for me. How am I supposed to do that?" (Calibrated question)

Dealer: "Well, that's the market price for this model."

Client: "I understand you need to make a profit..." (Showing empathy) "...but my budget is really tight right now." (Revealing legitimate constraints)

Dealer: "Let me talk to my manager and see what we can do."

The dealer returned with a $1,200 reduction—much better than the client would likely have achieved through traditional haggling.

This example illustrates how asking calibrated questions and showing empathy shifted the dynamic from confrontation to collaboration.

Preparing for a Negotiation

Effective negotiation begins long before you sit down at the table. A thorough preparation process includes:

★ Defining Your Objectives:

- ○ What is your ideal outcome?
- ○ What is your walk-away point (BATNA - Best Alternative To a Negotiated Agreement)?
- ○ What are your must-haves versus nice-to-haves?

★ Understanding the Other Side:

- ○ What are their likely interests and priorities?
- ○ What constraints might they be operating under?
- ○ What is their BATNA?

★ Creating Value:

- ○ What trade-offs might be possible?
- ○ Are there any creative solutions that could satisfy both parties?
- ○ Can you expand the pie before dividing it?

★ Preparing Your Communication:

- What tone do you want to set?
- How will you open the negotiation?
- What calibrated questions will you ask?

Exercise: Negotiation Preparation Worksheet

For your next negotiation, complete this worksheet:

1) My top three priorities are:

   a) _____

   b) _____

   c) _____

2) My walk-away point is: _____

3) The other party's likely priorities are:

   a) _____

   b) _____

   c) _____

4) Potential areas of mutual gain:

   a) _____

   b) _____

5) Three calibrated questions I will ask:

   a) _____

   b) _____

   c) _____

Key Negotiation Techniques from Chris Voss

1. **Use "No" to Start Negotiation, Not End It:** "No" often means "Wait" or "I'm not ready." When you hear "no," probe deeper to understand the underlying concerns.

2. **Trigger "That's Right" Moments:** When someone says "that's right," it indicates they feel genuinely understood. Summarize their position until you get this response.

3. **Beware of "Yes":** Early, eager agreement often indicates counterfeit compliance. Be skeptical of quick "yes" responses.

4. **Use the Power of "How":** Instead of saying "no" directly, ask "How am I supposed to do that?" to encourage the other side to solve your problem.

5. **Embrace Strategic Silence:** After asking a question or hearing a proposal, remain silent. People uncomfortable with silence often make concessions or reveal information.

6. **Identify Black Swans:** Look for the unknown unknowns—the pieces of information that, once revealed, completely change the negotiation dynamic.

Handling Difficult Negotiations and Dirty Tactics

Even with the best preparation, you may encounter challenging situations or manipulative tactics. Here's how to address them:

1. **When Faced with Aggression:** Acknowledge the emotion without accepting the position. "I can see you're frustrated. Let's take a step back and see what we're trying to accomplish here."

2. **When Faced with Deception:** Ask questions that require specific answers rather than making accusations.

3. **When Faced with Ultimatums:** Treat them as aspirations rather than true walk-away points. Respond with curiosity rather than counter-ultimatums.

4. **When Negotiations Stall:** Change the setting, take a break, or introduce a new element to the discussion.

Remember, maintaining your composure is often your greatest asset in difficult negotiations.

Reflection Questions:

1. *Think of a recent negotiation. How might the techniques we've discussed have improved the outcome?*

2. *What is your typical negotiation style? How could incorporating tactical empathy enhance your effectiveness?*

3. *What's one specific negotiation skill you could practice in the next month?*

As we continue our leadership journey, let's remember that negotiation is not just a skill for formal business deals—it's a daily practice that helps us navigate conflicts, build relationships, and create value in all areas of life. By mastering the art of negotiation, we equip ourselves to find solutions that benefit all parties and build the foundation for long-term success.

In the words of Chris Voss, *"Negotiation is not an act of battle; it's a process of discovery. The goal is to uncover as much information as possible."* Through this process of discovery, we not only achieve better outcomes but also build stronger relationships and more collaborative teams.

Part 5:

Personal Development and Philosophy

Week 47 - Essentialism and Focusing on the Vital Few (Greg McKeown)

"If you don't prioritize your life, someone else will." - Greg McKeown

In our previous chapters, we explored the importance of adaptability and leading through change, but here we shift gears to personal development and philosophy—the foundation for sustainable leadership and a fulfilling life. We begin this journey with *Essentialism: The Disciplined Pursuit of Less* by Greg McKeown, a powerful framework for cutting through the noise and focusing on what truly matters. At its heart, essentialism is about doing less, but better.

Understanding Essentialism

Essentialism is not about getting more things done. Instead, it's about getting the **right** things done. It's a disciplined, systematic approach to discerning what is essential, eliminating what is not, and creating space for what really matters. McKeown's philosophy is based on the principle that **our time, energy, and resources are finite**, and that only by focusing on a few vital priorities can we achieve meaningful success.

The essentialist thinks differently:

1. **They prioritize ruthlessly:** Instead of saying "yes" to everything, they say "no" to most things so they can say "yes" to the right things.
2. **They explore deliberately:** Essentialists don't rush into action. They pause, think, and carefully select where to focus their energy.
3. **They act purposefully:** Once a priority is clear, they execute it with concentration and excellence.

The Core Mindsets of Essentialism

To embrace essentialism, you need to adopt three core mindsets:

1. **Less, but better:**

   - Essentialists believe that **not everything is important**, and most things are trivial. They focus their effort on the few tasks that will have the greatest impact.
   - This shifts your mindset from "I have to do everything" to "What is the most valuable thing I can do?"

2. **The power of choice:**

- We often feel like we don't have control over our time or obligations. However, essentialism teaches us that saying "yes" to one thing means saying "no" to something else. By proactively choosing where to invest your energy, you regain control of your attention.
- *Key Question:* Where are you unintentionally giving away your power to choose?

3. **Trade-offs are unavoidable:**

   - Every decision has an opportunity cost. Instead of trying to have it all, essentialists embrace trade-offs and consciously decide what they're willing to give up in pursuit of the bigger goal.

Try This:

The Process of Becoming an Essentialist

McKeown outlines a step-by-step framework for adopting essentialism, which can be summarized in three main actions:

1. Explore: What is vital?
- Ask tough questions to determine what is truly important:
  - *What am I deeply passionate about?*
  - *What generates the highest return on my investment of time and energy?*
  - *What aligns with my purpose and values?*
- This requires intentional reflection and a willingness to evaluate your commitments.

Exercise: Write down everything you're currently working on or committed to (work, personal, family, social obligations). Then ask yourself: *If I could only focus on 1-2 of these, which would I choose? Why?*

2. Eliminate: What can I remove?
- Once you've identified the vital few priorities, the next step is to eliminate anything non-essential.

- This includes saying "no" to seemingly good opportunities that dilute your focus.
- McKeown suggests practicing "the graceful no"—polite but firm refusals that help maintain boundaries.

Exercise: Identify one commitment or project you need to eliminate today. Write exactly how you will say no, and practice this response if necessary.

3. *Execute: How can I make it effortless?*

- Essentialism is not just about choosing what to focus on but about creating systems and routines that make following through easier.
- Reduce friction in your life by automating, delegating, or simplifying tasks. Design an environment that supports focus and eliminates distractions.

Example: If your priority is health, make meal prep easy by pre-purchasing healthy groceries or preparing meals in bulk.

The Reality of Living as an Essentialist

Essentialism is simple in theory, but difficult in practice. It often means going against societal pressures and expectations. In a culture that glorifies busyness, saying "no" and focusing on fewer things can feel uncomfortable. However, the benefits are transformative:

1. **Increased clarity:** You stop being overwhelmed by everything on your plate and focus on what truly matters.
2. **Better results:** By dedicating yourself to fewer but higher-impact efforts, you achieve more meaningful success.
3. **Reduced stress:** Letting go of non-essentials frees your energy for the things that bring you joy and fulfillment.

Case Study: Steve Jobs When Steve Jobs returned to Apple in 1997, the company was producing a wide array of products. Jobs famously slashed Apple's product line from over 350 products to just 10 core offerings. The result? Apple became laser-focused on what mattered, leading to iconic innovations like the iPod, iPhone, and iPad.

This illustrates the power of ruthless prioritization: fewer products, but better ones.

Practical Tips for Embracing Essentialism

1. **Set boundaries:**

   - Learn to say no to requests that don't align with your priorities.
   - Example: If invited to a meeting, ask, "Is my attendance essential, or can I review afterward?"

2. **Schedule downtime:**

   - Essentialism requires time for reflection and recovery. Block out regular periods for thinking, planning, and rest.

3. **Adopt a "zero-based" mindset:**

   - Pretend all your commitments and projects are wiped out. Which ones would you re-add to your life if you were starting fresh?

4. **Conduct regular "priority audits":**

   - Revisit your goals and commitments every quarter to ensure they align with your vision.

5. **Eliminate distractions:**

   - Turn off notifications, create a workspace free of clutter, and set specific hours for deep work.

Reflection Questions

1. *Which of your current commitments feel essential? Which feel like distractions?*

2. *What is one area of your life where you could implement McKeown's principle of "less, but better"?*

3. *How can you shift your mindset to embrace the power of choice and make trade-offs intentionally?*

Final Thoughts: The Freedom of Essentialism

Essentialism is not about doing less just for the sake of doing less. It's about clearing away noise and clutter so you can give your attention to what truly matters. It's about making your highest contribution to your work, your relationships, and the world.

As Greg McKeown writes, "Only once you give yourself permission to stop trying to do it all, to stop saying yes to everyone, can you make your highest contribution toward the things that really matter."

This week, take a step back and reflect: *Are you doing your highest and best work? Or are you trying to do it all?*

By embracing essentialism, you can cultivate clarity, focus, and fulfillment—not through doing more, but through doing less, better.

Week 48 - Principles and Mental Models (Ray Dalio)

"Principles are fundamental truths that serve as the foundations for behavior that gets you what you want out of life." - *Ray Dalio*

In our previous chapter, we explored the power of Essentialism and the disciplined pursuit of the vital few. Now, we turn to **Principles** and **Mental Models**, with insights drawn from Ray Dalio's book *Principles* and frameworks from thinkers like Charlie Munger and Farnam Street. This chapter focuses on how to develop clear decision-making frameworks that align with your values and sharpen your ability to navigate complex challenges in life and leadership.

Understanding Principles

Ray Dalio defines principles as **fundamental truths** that serve as the foundation for how we think, act, and make decisions. They are not rigid rules but guiding philosophies that help us respond to situations consistently and effectively. Developing your own principles allows you to handle challenges with thoughtfulness, clarity, and objectivity, even in high-pressure situations.

Dalio learned the importance of principles through decades of leading Bridgewater Associates, one of the most successful hedge funds in the world. His approach emphasizes transparency, honesty, and radical truth-seeking. Whether navigating crises or making everyday choices, Dalio argues that **principled decision-making is the bedrock of success**.

Key Themes from *Principles*

Dalio's framework is rooted in a few key themes:

1. **Embrace Reality and Deal With It**

   - Face the world as it is, not as you wish it to be. Reject denial, and approach challenges with curiosity and a willingness to learn.
   - *Exercise*: Reflect on a recent setback. How did you respond? Did you approach it with an open mind, or did you resist facing reality?

2. **Be Radically Open-Minded**

   - Acknowledge that you don't know everything and seek out diverse perspectives to improve your decision-making.
   - This requires humility and the ability to listen actively, even to ideas you disagree with.

- *Quote from Dalio*: "If you're not failing, you're not pushing your limits, and if you're not pushing your limits, you're not maximizing your potential."

3. **Understand the 5-Step Process to Getting What You Want**
   Dalio's step-by-step process for achieving goals includes:

   - Set clear goals
   - Identify problems blocking your progress
   - Diagnose the root causes of those problems
   - Design a plan to overcome them
   - Execute the plan relentlessly

4. **Build a Machine**

   - View your life, team, or organization as a machine. Analyze it objectively, adjust it, and optimize it continuously for efficiency and effectiveness.

5. **Practice Radical Transparency**

   - Encourage open communication and the free flow of ideas in your workplace or team. Honest feedback, even when uncomfortable, enables better decision-making and stronger relationships.

What Are Mental Models?

If principles guide *how* we act, **mental models** guide *how* we think. Charlie Munger, Warren Buffett's business partner, defines mental models as frameworks for understanding how the world works. By mastering key mental models, you can improve your thinking, avoid cognitive biases, and make better decisions.

Munger advocates for a "latticework of mental models," meaning you should develop a broad understanding of key models from various disciplines—economics, psychology, biology, etc.—and apply them to the challenges you face.

Essential Mental Models for Leaders

Here are key mental models to help you think critically and make better decisions:

1. **First Principles Thinking (Physics)**

   - Break problems down to their fundamental truths and build up from there. Don't rely on assumptions or conventional wisdom.
   - *Example*: Elon Musk used first principles thinking to reimagine the cost of rockets at SpaceX by questioning why components had to be so expensive.

2. **The Pareto Principle (Economics)**

   - Also known as the 80/20 rule: 80% of results often come from 20% of efforts. Identify the 20% of tasks, clients, or activities that yield the greatest impact, and focus your energy there.

3. **Opportunity Cost (Economics)**

   - Every decision has a cost: what you forgo by choosing one option over another. This mental model encourages you to evaluate the true trade-offs of your decisions.

4. **Inversion (Mathematics)**

   - Instead of asking, "How can I succeed?" ask "What might cause me to fail?" Anticipating obstacles and avoiding mistakes often leads to better outcomes.

5. **Confirmation Bias (Psychology)**

   - Be aware of the tendency to seek information that confirms your beliefs while ignoring evidence to the contrary. Embrace opposing viewpoints to refine your thinking.

6. **Second-Order Thinking (Systems Thinking)**

   - Don't just consider the immediate consequences of a decision. Think about the ripple effects and unintended outcomes.
   - *Example*: Offering a discount might increase short-term sales, but what are the long-term impacts on pricing expectations and brand perception?

7. **The Circle of Competence (Business)**

   - Focus on your core strengths and expertise. Avoid overreaching into areas where you lack knowledge.

Try This:

Applying Principles and Mental Models in Leadership

1. **Clarify Your Core Values**

   - What principles matter most to you? Write down 3-5 core values that guide your behavior. For example:
     - Transparency
     - Growth through failure
     - Empowering others

2. **Create a Decision-Making Playbook**

   - Develop principles and mental models tailored to recurring decisions in your work or life. For example, if you frequently deal with hiring, your playbook might include:
     - *Principle*: Hire for cultural fit as much as for skills.
     - *Mental Model*: Use second-order thinking to evaluate how a new hire might impact team dynamics over time.

3. **Encourage Your Team to Adopt Principles**

   - Share your principles with your team and encourage them to create their own. This builds clarity, alignment, and mutual understanding around decision-making processes.

Exercise: **Create Your Own Principles**

1. Identify a major challenge or recurring problem in your work.
2. Write one guiding principle that would help you navigate that challenge more effectively.
3. Test that principle in your next decision-making process.

Real-Life Application: Bridgewater's Radical Transparency

Ray Dalio implemented radical transparency at Bridgewater Associates by recording all meetings and making them accessible to employees. This practice not only cultivated trust but also improved decision-making by giving everyone access to the same information.

While such a practice might not suit every organization, the underlying principle is universal: Transparency builds an open, collaborative culture that thrives on truth and accountability.

Reflection Questions

1. *What are 3 guiding principles that you live by? How do they influence your daily decisions?*

2. *Which mental model resonates with you most? How could you apply it to a current challenge?*

3. *How can you encourage your team, colleagues, or clients to adopt principles or mental models to improve their decision-making?*

Final Thoughts: Building a Latticework of Principles and Models

Leadership is not about making perfect decisions—it's about creating a strong foundation for consistent, thoughtful decision-making. By developing principles and expanding your knowledge of mental models, you increase your ability to navigate complexity and uncertainty with clarity and confidence.

In the words of Ray Dalio, *"Principles are the way you successfully deal with reality to get what you want out of life."* Combine these principles with the mental models that power your thinking, and you'll unlock extraordinary potential for both yourself and those you lead.

This week, take the opportunity to reflect on the principles and models that guide your decisions. Which ones are serving you well, and which ones might need refining? By committing to this practice of self-awareness and intentionality, you'll not only make better decisions but also create a legacy of thoughtful leadership.

Week 49 - Stoicism and the Art of Living (Ryan Holiday)

"You have power over your mind—not outside events. Realize this, and you will find strength."- Marcus Aurelius

In our previous chapter, we explored the importance of principles and mental models for mastering decision-making and leadership. Now, we delve into a philosophy that has stood the test of time: **Stoicism**—a way of thinking that equips us with resilience, clarity, and emotional fortitude in the face of life's challenges. Drawing on the insights of Ryan Holiday, author of *The Daily Stoic* and *The Obstacle Is the Way*, as well as ancient Stoic philosophers like Marcus Aurelius, Seneca, and Epictetus, this chapter focuses on how Stoicism can empower us to lead and live with purpose.

What Is Stoicism?

Stoicism is an ancient Greek philosophy that teaches us how to live a good life by focusing on what we can control, letting go of what we can't, and cultivating virtue as the ultimate goal. It's not just an abstract philosophy—it's a practical framework for managing emotions, overcoming adversity, and maintaining inner peace in a chaotic world.

The core idea of Stoicism can be summed up in this principle:
"It's not what happens to you, but how you respond that matters."

The Four Cardinal Virtues of Stoicism

Stoicism revolves around four key virtues, which guide how we think and act:

1. **Wisdom:** The ability to discern what is right and true and to make good decisions.

    - Wisdom teaches us to avoid rash judgments and to think critically before acting.

2. **Courage:** The strength to face challenges, hardship, and fear with resolve.

    - Courage is about doing what's right, even when it's difficult, and confronting adversity with resilience.

3. **Temperance:** The practice of self-control, discipline, and moderation.

    - Temperance helps us avoid overindulgence and impulsive actions that lead to regret.

4. **Justice:** Treating others fairly and acting with integrity.

- Justice emphasizes our responsibility to contribute to the well-being of others and society as a whole.

Together, these virtues form the foundation of Stoic philosophy and practical living.

Key Philosophical Concepts of Stoicism

1. Focus on What You Can Control

The Stoics teach us to separate what is within our control (thoughts, actions, attitudes) from what is outside our control (external events, other people's opinions, outcomes).

- **What's in your control:** Your thoughts, reactions, choices, and effort.
- **What's not in your control:** Other people's behavior, the past, the future, and random events.

Try This: Control Exercise

Write down a challenge you are currently facing. Divide it into two categories:

1. What you can control.
2. What you cannot control.

Commit to letting go of the latter and focusing only on actions within your control.

2. Turning Obstacles Into Opportunities

One of the most famous Stoic principles, popularized by Ryan Holiday in *The Obstacle Is the Way*, is the idea that obstacles are not roadblocks—they are pathways to growth. Challenges force us to develop new skills, perspectives, and strengths we wouldn't gain otherwise.

Try This: Reframe a Setback

Quote: "The impediment to action advances action. What stands in the way becomes the way." – Marcus Aurelius

Exercise: Reflect on a recent setback. Reframe it as an opportunity. Ask yourself:

- What did I learn from this experience?
- How has this challenge made me stronger or wiser?

3. Memento Mori – Remember You Will Die

The Stoics often reminded themselves of the inevitability of death—not to be morbid, but to keep life in perspective and inspire gratitude for the present moment. By reflecting on our mortality, we gain clarity on what truly matters and let go of trivial concerns.

Try This: What matters?

Write down your priorities for the next month.

Imagine this month was your last—would those priorities change?

Focus your energy accordingly.

4. Amor Fati – Love Your Fate

Amor Fati (Latin for "love of fate") is the Stoic principle of embracing everything that happens, whether good or bad, as necessary and meaningful. Instead of resisting reality, you accept it fully and learn to grow from it—even in hardship.

Try This: Love where you are

"A blazing fire makes flame and brightness out of everything that is thrown into it." – Marcus Aurelius

- Think about a challenging situation in your life. Write it down.

- How can you reframe it as something that is happening *for* you, not *to* you?

5. The Dichotomy of Control

Epictetus emphasized the importance of distinguishing between what you can influence and what you cannot. Worrying about uncontrollable factors only creates anxiety—focus all your energy on your actions and choices instead.

Stoicism in Leadership

For leaders, Stoicism provides a powerful toolkit for navigating uncertainty, managing emotions, and inspiring others. As a leader:

1. **Stay Calm Under Pressure**
   By controlling your emotions and responding thoughtfully, you create stability for your team—even in crises.

2. **Model Resilience**
   When you view challenges as opportunities, you inspire your team to see adversity in the same light.

3. **Practice Rational Decision-Making**
   Wisdom allows leaders to make decisions based on objective truths, not fear or impulse.

4. **Lead With Integrity**
   Justice and temperance ensure your actions are fair, measured, and aligned with your values.

5. **Cultivate Empathy**
   The Stoic virtue of justice teaches leaders to prioritize the well-being of others and act in the best interest of their teams.

Case Study: Marcus Aurelius

Here's one that Marcus Aurelius, the Roman emperor and author of Meditations, dealt with constant wars, political unrest, and personal tragedies—but his writings reveal a leader who maintained clarity, humility, and grace despite these challenges. His Stoic philosophy shaped how he responded to crises:

Focus on his role: Marcus embraced the responsibilities of leadership, even when they were difficult.
Temperance: He avoided indulgence and kept his life simple.
Amor Fati: Marcus accepted challenges as opportunities to live virtuously.

The timeless wisdom in Meditations remains one of the greatest examples of Stoic leadership and resilience.

Try This:

For the next week, try to accomplish these tasks each day.

Practical Ways to Practice Stoicism

1. **Daily Reflection:**

   - At the start of each day, ask yourself: *What challenges might I face today? How will I respond with wisdom and self-control?*
   - At the end of each day, reflect: *What did I handle well? What could I improve tomorrow?*

2. **Create a Dichotomy of Control List:**

   - Divide your current worries into two categories: controllable and uncontrollable. Let go of the latter.

3. **Limit Negative Thoughts:**

   - Use cognitive reframing to turn negative events into learning opportunities.

4. **Meditate on Memento Mori:**

   - Spend 5 minutes reflecting on mortality. Use this exercise to prioritize what truly matters in your life.

Reflection Questions

1. *How might embracing the Stoic principles of focusing on what you can control improve your leadership and decision-making?*

2. *What obstacles are currently in your way? How can they become opportunities for growth?*

3. *Which of the Stoic virtues—wisdom, courage, temperance, or justice—do you want to cultivate more intentionally in your life?*

Final Thoughts: Living the Stoic Way

Stoicism is not about suppressing emotions or denying challenges—it's about cultivating resilience, practicing gratitude, and living with virtue. This ancient philosophy offers practical tools for thriving in an unpredictable world and leading with integrity, clarity, and strength.

As Ryan Holiday writes, *"Stoicism is a tool in the pursuit of self-mastery, perseverance, and wisdom. It is not a philosophy for the passive. It is a philosophy for the people who run into problems in life and use them as fuel to get better."*

This week, challenge yourself to embrace the Stoic mindset: Focus on what you can control, reframe obstacles as opportunities, and live a life guided by wisdom, courage, temperance, and justice. Through this practice, you'll not only lead with resilience but also inspire others to do the same.

Week 50 - Logotherapy and Finding Meaning (Viktor Frankl)

"Everything can be taken from a man but one thing: the last of the human freedoms—to choose one's attitude in any given set of circumstances, to choose one's own way." – Viktor Frankl

In our previous chapter, we explored Stoicism and the art of resilience, a philosophy deeply tied to maintaining perspective and inner calm amidst life's challenges. This week, we turn to *Logotherapy*, a profound psychological framework introduced by Viktor Frankl in his timeless work *Man's Search for Meaning*. Frankl's insights on finding meaning in life, even in the face of great suffering, provide a foundation not only for personal resilience but also for purposeful leadership.

In this chapter, we examine how discovering and embracing meaning can empower you to lead a more intentional, focused, and fulfilling life, while also inspiring those around you to do the same.

What is Logotherapy?

Logotherapy, developed by Viktor Frankl, is a school of psychotherapy that is centered on the belief that the primary human drive is not pleasure (as Freud suggested) or power (as Adler proposed), but **the pursuit of meaning**. Frankl believed that even in the most challenging circumstances, we can find purpose, and it is this sense of purpose that sustains us.

Where Stoicism teaches us to focus on what we can control, Logotherapy teaches us that **meaning can be found in even the most difficult situations if we choose to find it.**

Frankl developed this philosophy during and after his harrowing experiences in Nazi concentration camps, where he observed that those who survived were often sustained by their connection to a purpose greater than themselves—even in the direst conditions.

The Three Pillars of Logotherapy

Frankl identified three primary ways to discover meaning in life:

1. **Meaning Through Work (Creating):**

    - Pursuing meaningful goals, projects, or contributions can give life purpose.

- *Exercise*: Reflect on your current work. How does it align with your sense of meaning? If it doesn't, how can you shift your focus toward work that feels purposeful?

2. **Meaning Through Relationships (Loving):**

   - Meaning can be found by fostering deep connections with others or by dedicating yourself to the well-being of loved ones.
   - Frankl observed that many prisoners in the concentration camps found strength in imagining themselves reunited with loved ones or dedicating their efforts to their memory.
   - *Exercise*: Who or what do you care most deeply about? How can you show that through your actions today?

3. **Meaning Through Suffering (Growing):**

   - Suffering, while undesirable, can be a powerful catalyst for growth if approached with the right mindset. When we accept suffering as a part of life and seek to grow through it, we find resilience and meaning.

   - Frankl wrote, *"When we are no longer able to change a situation, we are challenged to change ourselves."*

   - *Exercise*: Reflect on a past challenge or hardship. What did you learn or gain from the experience? How did it shape your sense of purpose?

The Existential Vacuum: The Danger of a Life Without Meaning

Frankl warned of the "existential vacuum"—a feeling of emptiness or purposelessness that arises when we lack meaning in our lives. In today's fast-paced world, this is increasingly common, often manifesting as boredom, burnout, apathy, or a reliance on distractions to fill the void.

To avoid falling into this trap:

- Regularly take time to reflect on your purpose and values.
- Pursue activities that align with your intrinsic motivations rather than external pressures.
- Look for opportunities to contribute to something larger than yourself—through work, relationships, or service to others.

Try This:

Leading with a Sense of Meaning

As a leader, your ability to connect with meaning has a profound impact on those you lead. People don't just want to work for a paycheck; they want to work for a purpose. Leaders who inspire others to find meaning in their work foster higher engagement, stronger loyalty, and greater resilience within their teams.

Steps to Inspire Meaning in Your Team:

1. **Share Your "Why":**

   - Be transparent about the meaning behind your work and how it contributes to a greater purpose.
   - *Example*: Simon Sinek's *Start with Why* highlights how organizations that connect their work to a deeper mission—like Apple revolutionizing technology or Patagonia advancing sustainability—attract more committed employees and customers.

2. **Clarify the Connection:**

   - Help individuals see how their roles contribute to the organization's mission. Show them that their work matters.

3. **Celebrate the Impact:**

   - Highlight the positive outcomes of your team's work, whether it's satisfied customers, business growth, or meaningful results in the community.

4. **Foster Empathy and Connection:**

   - Encourage collaboration and relationship-building so that team members feel connected to each other as well as the mission.

Case Study: Viktor Frankl in the Concentration Camps

Frankl's own life provides a remarkable illustration of Logotherapy in action. During his time in Auschwitz and other concentration camps, he faced unimaginable deprivation and suffering. Yet, he found meaning by:

1. **Imagining His Future Contribution:**

   - Frankl envisioned himself surviving the camps and sharing the lessons he had learned about finding meaning with the world.

2. **Focusing on Love:**

   - Frankl drew strength from imagining his wife and from the moments of human kindness he witnessed, even in the camps.

3. **Choosing His Response:**

   - While he could not control his external circumstances, he chose to control his inner response. By maintaining a sense of dignity and purpose, he preserved his humanity.

Frankl's ability to find meaning in suffering not only helped him survive but also enabled him to create a philosophy that has inspired millions.

Practical Ways to Apply Logotherapy

1. **Develop a Purpose Statement:**

   - Write down your personal mission or purpose in life. Use this as a compass to guide your decisions and actions.

2. **Reframe Challenges as Growth Opportunities:**

   - Instead of asking *"Why is this happening to me?"* ask, *"What can I learn from this?"*

3. **Practice Gratitude:**

- Regularly reflect on the people, opportunities, and moments that bring joy and meaning to your life.

4. **Engage in Meaningful Work:**

   - Identify how your work contributes to a greater goal or start seeking projects that align with your values.

5. **Help Others Find Meaning:**

   - Connect with others, mentor them, or contribute to causes you care about to create a ripple effect of purpose.

Reflection Questions

1. *What are the key sources of meaning in your life? How do they influence your decisions and priorities?*

2. *Reflect on a past hardship or period of suffering. How did it shape who you are today?*

3. *How can you help your team, family, or community find meaning in their work or lives?*

Final Thoughts: Living a Purposeful Life

Viktor Frankl's philosophy reminds us that meaning is not something we "find" passively—it is something we actively create by choosing how to respond to our circumstances. Whether through work, relationships, service, or even suffering, we have the power to infuse our lives with purpose.

As Frankl wrote, *"Life is never made unbearable by circumstances, but only by lack of meaning and purpose."*

This week, challenge yourself to reflect on your own sources of meaning. What drives you, and how can you align your actions more closely with your purpose? By living a life infused with meaning, you not only transform yourself but also inspire those around you to live with intention and resilience.

Week 51 - The Slight Edge and Compound Effect (Jeff Olson)

"The difference between successful people and unsuccessful people is the decisions they make every day." - Jeff Olson

As we approach the final chapters of our leadership journey, we shift focus to one of life's most powerful but often underestimated forces: **the power of small, consistent actions over time**. In this chapter, we explore the principles of *The Slight Edge* by Jeff Olson and *The Compound Effect* by Darren Hardy. Both of these books emphasize how seemingly insignificant daily habits and choices, when compounded, drive extraordinary results in life, leadership, and success.

This chapter is about taking control of your choices, embracing consistency, and recognizing that success isn't built in grand, sporadic leaps—it's built in small, intentional steps repeated over time.

The Core Idea: The Slight Edge and Compound Effect

The central idea of both *The Slight Edge* and *The Compound Effect* is simple but profound:

- **Small actions consistently repeated over time lead to massive results.**
- Conversely, small poor choices or missed opportunities, when compounded, lead to decline and failure.

These principles apply to every area of life—health, wealth, relationships, career, and personal growth. The key is recognizing that the small, daily decisions you make either move you closer to your goals or pull you further away from them.

Key Principles from *The Slight Edge*

Jeff Olson explains that success is not the result of dramatic wins or lucky breaks but of **consistent, simple actions done repeatedly over time**.

1. **Simple Things Are Easy to Do—and Easy Not to Do**

- The actions that lead to success are often simple, like reading 10 pages of a book daily, exercising for 30 minutes, or saving a small percentage of your income.
- However, these actions are also easy to neglect because their results are not immediately noticeable.

Example: Eating a healthy meal today won't instantly make you fit, and skipping it won't instantly make you unhealthy—but over time, these choices compound into vastly different outcomes.

Action Step: Identify one simple habit that aligns with your goals. Commit to doing it consistently for 30 days.

2. **The Power of Time and Consistency**

   - Small improvements might not seem significant in the moment, but over time, their impact becomes exponential.
   - *Quote:* "Success doesn't happen in a day; it happens in the daily."

Exercise: Think of an area in your life where you want to improve. What could you do daily, even if it's just for 5 minutes, to make progress over time?

3. **Momentum Is Built, Not Found**

   - Success in life isn't about making a single, massive leap. It's about showing up every day and doing the work, even when you don't see immediate results.

Example: Writing a book isn't about sudden bursts of inspiration but about dedicating time to write just a few hundred words every day.

Try This: Find Compoundable Actions

Darren Hardy builds on a similar foundation, emphasizing how small behaviors, repeated consistently, lead to life-altering transformations.

1. **Choices Shape Your Future**

- Life is the result of your choices. Major successes or failures don't come from one decision—they come from the accumulation of countless small decisions over time.
- *Example*: Spending $5 on coffee daily might seem insignificant, but over a year, that's over $1,800—a sum that could be invested instead.

Exercise: Track your daily habits for a week. Notice which small, repeated actions are moving you closer to your goals and which might be holding you back.

2. **The Magic of Habits**

   - Habits are the building blocks of success. Once positive habits are in place, they create momentum that carries you forward.
   - Hardy recommends starting small and being consistent. Over time, these small habits snowball into life-transforming results.

3. **Tracking the Compound Effect**

   - Measuring your progress reinforces positive behavior. Keeping track of your actions, no matter how small, builds accountability and motivation.

   Example: If your goal is to improve your fitness, track the number of steps you take daily or the number of workouts completed each week.

Why Small Choices Are So Powerful

In the moment, small actions may not seem to matter. Skipping a workout today or spending an extra hour on social media might not feel significant—but over time, the accumulated effects of such decisions can be life-changing.

- **Positive Choices:** Daily effort adds up. Reading a chapter of a self-development book or taking 20 minutes to learn a new skill each day might seem minor—but imagine the impact of 365 small improvements over the course of a year.

- **Negative Choices:** Conversely, habits like procrastination, unhealthy eating, or avoiding difficult conversations, when compounded, can significantly decrease your quality of life over time.

The Ripple Effect of Consistency

One of the most exciting aspects of the slight edge and compound effect is how they create ripple effects in other areas of your life.

1. **Health:** Starting with a small fitness habit like walking 10 minutes daily can lead to more energy, better sleep, and increased productivity.
2. **Finances:** Saving just $5 a day can grow into significant savings or investments over the years.
3. **Relationships:** Spending quality time with a loved one daily strengthens bonds and deepens trust.
4. **Personal Growth:** Reading or learning a new skill regularly opens doors to new opportunities and insights.

Building Your Slight Edge Habits

To leverage the slight edge, follow these steps:

1. **Clarify Your Goals:**

   - Define the long-term outcomes you want in different areas of your life (e.g., health, career, relationships).
   - *Example Goal:* "I want to run a half marathon in the next year."

2. **Identify Simple Daily Actions:**

   - Break down your goals into small, achievable habits.
   - *For a marathon goal, this might include:* Running 1 mile daily or committing to 20 minutes of training 5 times per week.

3. **Track Your Progress:**

   - Use tools like journals, apps, or spreadsheets to monitor your consistency.
   - Seeing daily wins builds motivation and reinforces the habit.

4. **Start Small and Build:**

- Don't try to overhaul all areas of your life at once. Focus on just 1-2 small changes until they become habits, then add new ones.

5. **Celebrate Small Wins:**

   - Acknowledge your progress. Small celebrations reinforce positive behavior and keep you motivated.

Real-Life Example: The Penny Doubling Theory

One of the most famous examples from *The Compound Effect* is the penny-doubling theory:

- Imagine choosing between $1 million upfront or a single penny that doubles in value every day for 31 days.
- While the penny seems insignificant at first, by day 31, its compounded value surpasses $10 million.

The lesson here is clear: small actions may seem insignificant at first, but over time, their impact can be monumental.

Reflection Questions

1. *What small, daily actions are contributing to your long-term goals? Which ones might be holding you back?*

2. *In what area of your life do you feel stuck? What small habit could you introduce to create momentum over time?*

3. *How can you inspire your team, family, or colleagues to embrace the power of small, consistent actions in their own lives?*

Final Thoughts: The Exponential Power of Small Decisions

Both *The Slight Edge* and *The Compound Effect* teach us that success is not about dramatic, life-altering moments but about the tiny, unremarkable decisions we make each day. The key is to stay consistent, even when the results aren't immediately visible, because over time, the compounding power of your efforts will create exponential growth.

As Jeff Olson writes, *"The choice is always yours. Every day, every hour, every moment, you get to choose the slight edge."*

This week, reflect on your daily habits. How are they shaping your future? By committing to small, purposeful actions today, you set the foundation for an extraordinary tomorrow.

Week 52 - Leaving a Legacy and Paying It Forward

"Carve your name on hearts, not tombstones. A legacy is etched into the minds of others and the stories they share about you."- Shannon L. Alder

As we reach the final chapter of this leadership journey, we turn to one of the most profound and lasting aspects of leadership and personal development: **leaving a legacy and paying it forward**. Leadership is not just about achieving personal success—it's about creating a ripple effect of positive impact that extends far beyond yourself. Whether through the teams you lead, the people you mentor, or the communities you serve, the mark you leave behind is the true measure of your success as a leader.

This week, we focus on the principles of building a legacy, inspiring others to carry forward your values and vision, and making contributions that will echo far into the future.

What Does It Mean to Leave a Legacy?

Leaving a legacy is not about monuments, fame, or fortune—it's about the ways in which your actions, values, and vision shape the lives of others. At its core, a legacy is about the impact you have on people. It's the wisdom you pass down, the opportunities you create, and the example you set for others to follow.

Key Questions to Reflect On:

1. How will people remember you when you're gone?
2. What values do you want to pass down to your family, team, or community?
3. What contributions will continue to make a difference after you're no longer here to see them?

The Two Dimensions of Legacy

Legacy exists in two dimensions: **personal legacy** and **professional legacy.**

1. Personal Legacy

Your personal legacy revolves around the relationships you build and the lives you touch. It's about how you're remembered by your family, friends, and community.

Examples:

- Instilling strong values in your children
- Being a mentor who helps others achieve their dreams
- Creating meaningful memories with loved ones

Exercise: Write down 3 core values you want to pass down to those closest to you. Reflect on how well your daily actions align with these values.

2. Professional Legacy

Your professional legacy is about the impact you make in your work, your leadership, and the contributions you leave behind for your industry or organization.

Examples:

- Building a company culture that prioritizes integrity and innovation
- Mentoring employees to become leaders in their own right
- Delivering solutions or projects that make lasting contributions to your clients or field

Exercise: Think about your current role or business. What will its long-term impact be, and how can you ensure that its positive influence continues after you're gone?

Try This: Legacy Building

Ways to Build a Legacy

1. Lead With Purpose

To leave a meaningful legacy, you must be intentional. Every decision, project, and interaction should align with your values and your long-term vision.

Reflection Question: What is the greater purpose behind your leadership? How do your daily actions reflect that purpose?

2. Empower Others

One of the most powerful ways to leave a legacy is to invest in the growth and success of others. This creates a ripple effect that extends your impact far beyond what you could accomplish alone.

Examples:

- Mentoring young leaders in your organization
- Sharing knowledge freely to help others succeed
- Delegating responsibilities and empowering your team to innovate

Exercise: Identify one person you could mentor or empower this month. What steps can you take to support their growth?

3. Pay It Forward

Just as others have paved the way for your success, you can pay it forward by opening doors for others, contributing to your community, and giving back.

Examples:

- Supporting charitable causes aligned with your values
- Offering opportunities to underprivileged individuals
- Sharing your time, resources, or skills for the benefit of others

Exercise: Identify one way you can give back this week—whether through mentorship, volunteering, or donations.

4. Create Something That Lasts

Legacies are often marked by tangible contributions—building something that outlives you and continues to provide value for future generations.

Examples:

- Writing a book filled with your insights and experiences
- Starting a nonprofit or initiative to address a societal need
- Contributing thought leadership to your industry

The Philosophy of Paying It Forward

Paying it forward is rooted in the idea that the positive impact you receive should be amplified and shared with others. It's about creating a chain reaction of kindness, generosity, and opportunity.

Examples in Leadership:

- Helping an employee grow into a leadership role
- Providing thoughtful advice to someone starting their career
- Offering support to someone who's struggling, with no expectation of reciprocity

The beauty of paying it forward is that its effects are exponential: each person you help will, in turn, be inspired to help others.

Case Study: Warren Buffett's Philanthropic Legacy

Warren Buffett, one of the most successful investors of all time, has committed to leaving the vast majority of his wealth to philanthropic causes through the Giving Pledge. Beyond his financial contributions, Buffett's legacy includes the principles of generosity, humility, and empowering others to create positive change.

Buffett's approach exemplifies the idea that leaving a legacy isn't just about the wealth or success you accumulate—it's about how you use those resources to make the world a better place.

Practical Steps to Leave a Legacy

1. **Define Your Legacy**

    - Take time to reflect on how you want to be remembered. Write down the values, relationships, and contributions that matter most to you.

2. **Act Consistently With Your Values**

- Ensure your daily actions align with the legacy you hope to leave.

3. **Create Opportunities for Others**

   - Empower your team, mentor individuals, and open doors for others to succeed.

4. **Give Back to Your Community**

   - Find ways to contribute to causes or initiatives that align with your values.

5. **Capture Your Insights**

   - Consider writing, speaking, or documenting your lessons for future generations.

6. **Build Systems That Outlive You**

   - Whether it's through your business, a nonprofit, or another venture, create lasting systems that amplify your impact over time.

Reflection Questions

1. *What relationships, values, or contributions will define the legacy you leave behind?*

2. *What opportunities can you create for others in your personal or professional life?*

3. *How can you pay forward the support or opportunities you've received?*

Final Thoughts: Your Leadership Legacy

Leaving a legacy isn't about achieving perfection—it's about living with intention and ensuring that the impact of your life and leadership echoes into the future. The actions you take today, the values you embody, and the relationships you nurture will form the foundation of your legacy.

In the words of Maya Angelou, *"Your legacy is every life you've ever touched."*

This week, take time to reflect on your values, your contributions, and the ripple effects of your leadership. By living with purpose and paying it forward, you can create a legacy that leaves the world better than you found it.